ARCO

OFFICE GUIDE TO BUSINESS LETTERS, MEMOS & REPORTS

LEONARD ROGOFF, Ph. D.

with

GRADY BALLENGER, Ph. D.

MACMILLAN • USA

W9-BKB-906

Macmillan General Reference
A Simon & Schuster Macmillan Company
1633 Broadway
New York, NY 10019-6785

An Arco Book

MACMILLAN is a registered trademark of Macmillan, Inc.
ARCO is a registered trademark of Prentice-Hall, Inc.

Library of Congress Cataloging in Publication Data

Rogoff, Leonard.
    Office guide to business letters, memos and reports /
  Leonard Rogoff, Grady Ballenger. —2nd ed.
      p. cm.
  ISBN 0-671-89664-4
   1. Commercial correspondence. 2. Memorandums.
  3. Business report writing. I. Ballenger, Grady. II. Title.
HF5726.R72   1994   94-25593
651.7'5—dc20   CIP

Manufactured in the United States of America

10 9 8

CONTENTS

FOREWORD

The *Office Guide to Business Letters, Memos, and Reports* offers models of standard business writing. Standard models are not inflexible, however, and writers should feel free to exercise personal judgment in adapting these examples to their own needs. Two basic rules: be consistent and use common sense.

Many firms, especially large ones, employ their own "house style." Other firms adhere to manuals published by various trade associations, newspapers, or university presses. Before starting on any business writing project, check to see if your company uses a particular style. You will want your work to reflect your company's policy.

Word processing and desktop publishing have opened new possibilities. Your company likely has preferences in its use of computer software, and you will need to learn these systems. The company's correspondence may follow a standard format that is already programmed in the computer, or you may choose from a variety of types and designs. The basic rule of business writing is still to keep the page as clean and easy to read as possible.

Your business letter, memo, or report conveys an image of your company to the outside world. Remember, too, it reflects your professional standards and competence.

STYLE

Make your points in the fewest possible words. Write clearly, avoiding jargon and wordiness. Try to use fresh language without resorting to clichés.

Wordiness

Wordiness involves the use of "dead" words which do not contribute to the meaning of a sentence. Certain commonly used phrases are wordy and should be reduced or omitted. For example:

wordy: I need your help *in order to* solve the problem.
better: I need your help *to* solve the problem.

wordy: Due to the fact that the merchandise was damaged, we are withholding payment.
better: Because the merchandise was damaged, we are withholding payment.

wordy: It is our opinion that the policy should be changed.
better: We feel that the policy should be changed.

1

Here is a list of wordy phrases with suggested corrections:

at a later date	later
despite the fact that	although
due to the fact that	because
for the purpose of	for, to
in addition	also
in a number of cases	some
in order that	so
in order to	to
in reference to	about
in terms of	as for
in the amount of	for, of
in the event of	if
in the near future	soon
in this day and age	now, today
in this regard	(delete)
in view of	because, since
it is our opinion that	we feel
on the occasion of	when
prior to	before
subsequent to	after
without further delay	immediately
with reference to	about
with respect to	about
would you please be so kind as to	please

Redundancy

Redundancy is a form of wordiness. Redundant words repeat rather than develop the point. To describe something as "brown in color" is redundant since brown implies color. For example:

> *redundant:* In *the year of 1994* retail sales dropped sharply.
> *better:* In *1994* retail sales dropped sharply.

> *redundant:* Suarez Mills is the *one and only* source of the fabric.
> *better:* Suarez Mills is the *only* source of the fabric.

> *redundant:* I enclose a check for *the amount of $378.25.*
> *better:* I enclose a check for *$378.25.*

Here are some redundant phrases with possible improvements:

agreeable and satisfactory	agreeable *or* satisfactory
and etc.	etc.
basic fundamentals	basics *or* fundamentals
completely perfect	perfect
consensus of opinion	consensus
each and every	each
first and foremost	first
follows after	follows
full and complete	full *or* complete
general consensus	consensus
honest and open	honest
hope and trust	hope *or* trust

if and when	if *or* when
in my personal opinion	in my opinion
insist and demand	insist *or* demand
meet together	meet
most unique	unique
one and only	only
prompt and speedy	prompt
repeats again	repeats
reverts back	reverts
right and proper	right *or* proper
sincere and earnest	sincere *or* earnest
thoughtful and considerate	thoughtful *or* considerate
true facts	facts
very unique	unique
willing and eager	willing *or* eager

Jargon

Jargon occurs when the writer uses excessively technical words—often very long ones—when simpler, shorter words would be more effective. Be wary of words that end in -ize, -tion, or -ity. Though writers of jargon try to demonstrate that they are authorities, they more often confuse the reader. For example:

> *jargon:* An enhanced commitment to a public relations effort remains a viable option for the firm.
> *better:* We may also wish to improve our public relations.

> *jargon:* The implementation of cost-cutting
> strategies can impact budgetary deficits.
> *better:* Cutting costs will reduce deficits.

Be especially sensitive to words that are used in computer language:

> *jargon:* I would appreciate hearing your *feedback*
> on the report.
> *better:* I would apreciate hearing your *response* to
> the report.

> *jargon:* We need to *interface* the departmental
> efforts.
> *better:* We need to *coordinate* the departmental
> efforts.

Jargon can often be corrected by using more concrete words. Here is a list of some jargon:

acknowledge receipt of
answer affirmatively, negatively
expend maximum effort
feedback
impact a problem
implement a decision
input
interface
proactive
remunerate

Clichés

Clichés are expressions that have lost their meaning through overuse. Rather than request a "100-percent effort," ask for "hard work." For example:

> *cliché:* In today's market we must *move forward or fall behind.*
> *better:* In today's market we must improve our efficiency.

> *cliché:* The Prostar is *just what you're looking for.*
> *better:* The Prostar will meet your word-processing needs.

Some other clichés:

allow me to	100-percent effort
along these lines	over the hill
do our utmost	pave the way
down but not out	sell like hot cakes
facts of life	short and sweet
for your information	slow but sure
keep abreast	to be perfectly honest
last but not least	touch all bases
latest developments	vicious circle
meet the eye	work like a dog
nip in the bud	

BUSINESS LETTERS

The business letter reflects the competence and professionalism of the person sending it. The quality of its contents and presentation is an advertisement for the company. Business letters should always be neat and easy to read. The format should be attractive and uncluttered. Always maintain a positive, courteous tone. The goal is to earn the goodwill of the person reading the letter.

Business letters will vary in format and content depending upon their purpose. The tone can be formal or informal depending on the occasion. A business letter may be an invitation for a golfing date to a friend or an application for employment to a large, impersonal corporation. Be sure to strike an appropriate tone.

Business letters in a company or an organization usually follow a consistent format. Check to see if your firm follows a particular manual or house style. Many computer software programs have defaults that will determine the width of margins, size and style of type fonts, ragged or justified (even) right margins, and so on. These defaults can be overridden, if necessary, to fit your company's house style.

Business letters can generally be broken down into three parts. A brief introductory paragraph states the reason for the letter, setting a courteous tone. The body of the letter, consisting of one or more paragraphs, develops the major point with ample supporting detail. The conclusion should be short, thanking the reader for his or her attention and suggesting possibilities for further action. If the message is very brief—a congratulatory note or confirmation of a meeting—these points may be condensed into a paragraph or two.

Before sending the letter, be sure to proofread it carefully. If using a word processor, you may wish to check spelling with the computerized dictionary. Proofreading should be done slowly, letter by letter. Several readings are often necessary to catch all potential problems.

Parts of a Business Letter

(See Model Letter on page 25)

Letterhead   (1)

Businesses usually have letterhead stationery, which contains the company's logo, name, address, telephone number, and other preprinted information. If the stationery is not letterhead, type the writer's address in the upper right-hand corner:

    Street
    City, State   ZIP

Do not use abbreviations for the street or city; the U. S. Postal Service two-letter state abbreviations may be used (see page 224).

Dateline   (2)

The date is typed at least three lines below the letterhead either on the left margin or on the right margin, depending on letter style. If the letter is brief, leave more spaces under the letterhead to give the letter a balanced appearance. If the stationery lacks a letterhead, type the date under the city and state of the writer's address.

Dates may follow several forms:

traditional	Month day, year May 27, 1994
science, military, government	day Month year 27 May 1994
informal, handwritten letters	month/day/year 5/27/94
informal (European style)	day/month/year 27/5/94

Mail Notation

If the letter has been sent by express mail, special delivery, certified or registered mail, a notation may be printed in capitals on the left margin. It may appear at the top of the letter two lines below the date or at the bottom of the letter two lines below the final typed line. Mail notations often are typed only on carbon copies.

(near the top of the letter)

839 Ridge Road
Rutherford, New Jersey 00000
May 27, 1994

CERTIFIED MAIL

Ms. Angela Torres
27 Snowtown Boulevard
Edina, Minnesota 00000

(near the bottom of the letter)

Yours truly,

Erica Jordan, President

EJ/hw
CERTIFIED MAIL

Confidential Notation

If the letter is to be read only by the addressee, type
PERSONAL or CONFIDENTIAL, in capitals, on the left
margin four lines under the date. If a mail notation
appears at the top, type the personal or confidential notation directly under it.

Inside Address (3)

The inside address, typed flush on the left margin, contains information about the person or company that receives the letter. It should conform to the address on the envelope. Usually, it consists of three parts:

Person or company
Street address
City, State ZIP

Use *Mr.*, *Mrs.*, *Ms.*, or *Dr.* before the person's name and, if it is short, the person's position in the company:

Mr. Max Lenowitz, Manager
Ms. Tanya Simmons, Supervisor

If the title is long, it may be placed under the name:

Mr. Max Lenowitz
District Sales Manager

Ms. Molly Lail
Personnel Supervisor

For ministers, medical doctors, and professionals who hold doctoral degrees, use either *Dr.* or *Doctor* before the name, *or* put the degree after the name:

Katherine Grady, Ph.D.
or
Doctor Katherine Grady

Reverend Thomas Leach, D. D.
or
Reverend Dr. Thomas Leach

The same principle holds true for lawyers who use *Esquire*:

Mr. John Curry
    or
John Curry, Esq.

Print the name of the company as it appears on the company's letterhead.

Angelo Bros. Candles
Smith & Guthridge
D. Mills Inc.

Avoid using abbreviations in the street, city, and state address except for official Postal Service codes.

Mr. Charles Huang, President
Home Office Systems
34 Stratford Place
Del Mar, CA 00000

Mr. Robert Kowalski
Vice-President of Operations
Castro Steel, Incorporated
3 Industrial Parkway
Gary, Indiana 00000

Attention Line   (4)

An attention line is frequently included in business letters that are addressed impersonally to a company. Such a letter may require the attention of a specific person, position, or division. Several styles are acceptable:

Attention: Mr. Malik Lipscomb
Attention: Mr. Malik Lipscomb, Sales Manager
Attention: Sales Manager
Attention of Sales Manager
ATTENTION Sales Division
ATTENTION—Mr. Malik Lipscomb

The attention line should appear two lines beneath the inside address. When using an attention line, omit the person's name from the inside address. Use an impersonal greeting—not the name on the attention line.

Drexler Electric Company
117 East Eighteenth Street
New York, NY 00000

Attention: Sales Division

Sir or Madam:

Salutation (5)

The salutation is the greeting to the reader of the letter. Use the name and title of the person listed in the inside address.

Dr. Gerald Royster
23 Charlotte Road
Topeka, Kansas 00000

Dear Dr. Royster

Salutations establish a relationship between the reader and the writer which can be either formal or informal. If you know the reader well and desire a casual tone, use an informal salutation. Official business correspondence usually requires a formal greeting, though the current trend is to be more informal. To be very formal, omit the personal *dear.*

Very formal	*Formal*
Sir:	Dear Dr. Royster
Madam:	Dear Ms. Johnson
Sir or Madam:	Dear Prof. Sekora:
Staff:	

Informal
Dear Gerry:
Dear Tony:
Dear Vitaly:

Use either the first name or the last name of the addressee in a salutation, not both. If you do not know whether a woman is a Miss or Mrs. use Ms. If you are unsure whether the person is a man or a woman you may use first and last names:

Dear Lee Jones:
Dear Jean LaFrance:

If you do not know who will be reading the letter, use a salutation that will include all possible readers. For this reason, use a greeting that does not define the reader's sex.

Dear Sir or Madam:
Dear Madam or Sir:
Dear Friend:
Dear Customer:
Dear Staff:

In standard punctuation, a colon is placed after the salutation in a business letter. A comma is used only in a personal letter. Some businesses use an open punctuation style which does not require a punctuation mark after the salutation. (Check the house style preferred by your business.)

Subject Line (6)

A subject line informs the reader briefly about the letter's contents. Many styles are acceptable:

Subject: Computer sales
SUBJECT: Inventory control
Subject—Revised Pricing Policy
Subject: New Credit Guidelines
Subject: Order No. 7176
CONTRACT NEGOTIATIONS

Some companies prefer to use the Latin word *re* (thing) in place of *subject:*

Re: Computer sales
RE: Inventory Control

The subject line is located two spaces directly under the salutation:

Dear Mr. Lee:

Subject: Computer sales

Dear Ms. Hernandez:

CONTRACT NEGOTIATIONS

Introduction (7)

The opening of a business letter should state the writer's purpose and set the tone for the letter. It should capture the reader's attention and establish a link between writer and reader. The opening should also be brief. Two or three lines is sufficient.

Compro offers a personal computer that can perform the desktop publishing functions that you have outlined in your letter of March 15. It is the Prostar 800. With a laser printer, it fits your price range.

Body (8)

The body of a business letter contains one or more paragraphs that provide detailed supporting facts or further explanation. These points should be developed logically, step-by-step and as clearly as possible. Include all necessary information—but no more—and maintain a positive tone.

The Prostar 800 was designed primarily for the home office. The company has been building computerized editorial equipment for over twenty years, and the Model 800 offers the most advanced technology available. The system can be configured to meet your specific needs for power and drives. All Prostar systems are easily expandable and upgradable. The Prostar 800 package includes Speedwrite and Smartbook, the two most popular programs in word processing and desktop publishing.

Conclusion (9)

The final paragraph of a business letter should end on a positive note; it should encourage the reader to respond favorably to the message of the letter. If possible, conclude with a personal remark, suggesting an appointment or expressing a desire for more communication.

I would be happy to meet with you at your convenience to answer any questions about the Prostar. Compro offers sales and service that can keep you up to date with the latest technology—at competitive prices. Please call me at 000-0000. I look forward to hearing from you.

Complimentary Close (10)

As does the salutation, the complimentary close reflects the relationship between writer and reader. Thus, the close should maintain the same tone as the salutation. If the salutation uses the reader's first name, choose an informal complimentary close and sign with the writer's first name. If you address the reader by the last name, a more formal complimentary close is usually appropriate.

Very formal Respectfully, Respectfully yours,	*Formal* Yours truly, Yours very truly, Very truly yours,
Informal Sincerely, Sincerely yours, Cordially, Cordially yours	*Very informal* Best, Best wishes, Regards,

Only the first word in a complimentary close is capitalized. The last word is followed by a comma.

The writer's name should be typed under the complimentary close, leaving three to five spaces for the signature.

Yours truly,   Cordially yours,
Emily Pratt   Frank Chan

The title of the writer may be added after the name—if the title is short. Separate the name and title by a comma or a hyphen.

Ginna Curry, Director

You may also list the writer's title after the name and then type the division or department under it.

Sal Mazza, Chairman
Department of Engineering

To emphasize that the company, rather than the signer, is responsible for the letter, the company's name may appear two lines under the complimentary close. The writer's name is typed four lines beneath that:

Yours truly,
Plaza Associates
Joseph Hassan, Vice-president

Identification Initials   (11)

Identification (or reference) initials indicate who wrote, dictated, and typed the letter. Usually, the writer's initials are typed in capitals followed by the secretary's initials. The identification initials are typed on the left margin two lines beneath the signature block. Several styles are acceptable:

LBR/as   LBR:as
LBR/AS   LBR:AS

Enclosures (12)

If other materials are included with the letter, add an enclosure notation on the left margin two lines below the identification initials or the signature block. The notation may be written out or abbreviated.

Enclosure
Enc.
Encl.

If you itemize the enclosures, a colon or dash may be added:

Enclosure:
Enclosure—

After the enclosure note, you may list the number of items that are included:

Encl. 2
Enclosures—2
Enclosures (2)
Enc. 2

If you include more than one enclosure or if the enclosures are important, list them by name.

Enclosures:	Encl.
Copyright Form	Check
Letter of Credit	Catalogue
Contract	Order Form

Copies

If copies are sent to other persons, a carbon copy notation is added two lines below the identification initials or enclosure notation, whichever is last. Several styles are acceptable:

    cc
    cc:
    CC
    CC:
    Copies to

You may list the initials, names, or names and addresses of those who receive copies.

    cc Dr. Jeremy Nord
       Mr. Gus Spelman
       Ms. Haley Saunders

    cc: JN
        GS
        HS

    Copies to Dr. Jeremy Nord
              213 Knightsbridge Way
              Asheville, NC 00000

    Copies to Mr. Gus Spelman
              31A Pirate Street
              Boston, MA 00000

If you do not want the reader of the letter to know that copies are being sent, then use a notation for blind carbon copy on the carbon sheets or copies only:

    bcc
    bcc:
    BCC
    BCC:

Postscripts

In business letters a postscript is used only to emphasize an important point, not to include information that was left out of the letter. In sales letters a postscript may be used to highlight a final selling point. Use one of the following abbreviations:

P.S. PS. PS: PS—

Postscripts are single-spaced two lines below the last notation.

P.S. If you order within ten days, I am authorized to offer a 10 percent discount.

Multi-page Letter

If possible, try to fit the contents of your letter onto one page; a one-page letter is easier to read and to handle than a multi-page letter. If the second page is only three or four lines long, try to include the information on the first page. With the possible exception of sales letters (unsolicited advertising especially), do not use the back of the page.

Do not use letterhead stationery for additional pages, but use paper of the same quality as the first page. Six spaces from the top of the second page, starting on the left-hand margin, type a heading to identify the letter.

Fazio Motors   -2-   August 19, 1994

Fazio Motors
Page 2
August 19, 1994

Fazio Motors
2
August 19, 1994

The text begins four lines below the heading.

Paper

Business letters should be written on high-quality paper.
Banks and law offices usually specify 100 percent rag
paper. A bond paper with a watermark is suitable for business use. For most business letters choose a 20-pound
weight, white bond paper. Twenty-four weight may be
used for important letters. For copies and overseas air
mail, six- to 13-pound weight is sufficient; these papers
are known as "tissue" or "onionskin."

Use	Size
General business correspondence	8$1/2$" X 11" or 8$1/2$" X 10$1/2$"
Executive stationery	7$1/2$" X 10$1/2$"
Notes and memos	5$1/2$" X 10$1/2$"

Typing Instructions

Spacing

Except for very short letters, business letters should be
single-spaced with double spaces between paragraphs.
Very short letters of 50 words or less may be double-
spaced (including addresses) with triple-spacing between
paragraphs. (Half-sheet paper 5$\frac{1}{2}$" X 8$\frac{1}{2}$", may be used
for short letters.)

A business letter should appear attractive and orderly.
To balance the text on the page, the number of spaces
between the letterhead, date, and inside address may vary
from two to six spaces.

Margins

The size of the margins is dictated by the length of the
letter. Try to balance the text in the center of the page.

Short letters	2-inch margins
Medium-length letters	1$\frac{1}{2}$-inch margins
Long letters	1-inch margins

Margins may be ragged or justified. A ragged margin will
be aligned on the left margin but not on the right margin:

> The typist must choose how to set the margins.
> Ragged margins leave more blank space
> on the page, often making it easier to read. The
> word-processing program may be set to
> "default" with a ragged margin.

A justified margin will be evenly aligned on the right as well as the left:

> With the use of word processors many typists prefer to justify the margins. It creates a neater, balanced look, especially with block style. Word-processing programs will wrap the text so that the right margin will be evenly aligned. This style is commonly used now.

Check, once again, to see if your company has a particular preference.

Model Business Letter

COMPANY LETTERHEAD

1 Street Address
City, State ZIP

(2-6 spaces)

2   Month day, year

(3-8 spaces)

Addressee, Title
3 Street Address
City, State ZIP

(2 spaces)

4 ATTENTION: LINE

(3 spaces)

5 Dear Addressee:

(2 spaces)

6 Subject: Typing Instructions

(2 spaces)

7 The text of a business letter is single-spaced with double spacing between paragraphs.

The left and right margins should be set as follows: two inches for short
8 letters; one and a half inches for medium-length letters; one inch for long letters.

9 The bottom margin should be at least one and a half inches or six lines.

(2 spaces)

Complimentary close,

10   (4-6 spaces for signature)

Writer's Name, Title

(2 spaces)

11 Initials

(1-2 spaces)

12 Enclosures

Letter Formats

Several formats are acceptable in typing the business letter: (1) block, (2) modified block, (3) modified semi-block, (4) simplified, and (5) indented. The trend today is toward simpler, less cluttered styles, using minimal punctuation. Check to see which style is preferred by your company.

Standard Punctuation

Standard punctuation (or mixed punctuation) is the most popular style. It is used with block, modified block, or modified semi-block styles. The salutation ends with a colon, and the complimentary close is followed by a comma. The dateline and addresses include interior punctuation, but no end punctuation is used.

June 6, 1994

Mr. Jose Pagano
Sterling Mortgage Company
16 Montross Court
Albuquerque, NM 00000

Dear Mr. Pagano:

Open Punctuation

Open punctuation is required for letters in simplified style; it is optional for block style. Salutations and complimentary closes may be eliminated, but if used, no punctuation follows. The comma is retained between the day and year in the dateline and between the city and state in addresses, but no punctuation appears at the end of the lines.

June 6, 1994

Mr. Jose Pagano
Sterling Mortgage Company
16 Montross Court
Albuquerque, NM 00000

Dear Mr. Pagano

Closed Punctuation

Closed punctuation is used mostly with the indented letter style. This style is not used in the United States but is still employed in Europe. Commas are placed at the end of each line in the address—except for the last, which ends with a period. A period also follows the dateline. The salutation is followed by a colon, and commas are placed at the end of each line of the complimentary close, signature block, and notations. A period is placed at the end of the signature block and notations.

BLOCK STYLE

COMPANY LETTERHEAD
Street
City, State ZIP

Month day, year

Addressee, Title
Company
Street Address
City, State ZIP

ATTENTION NAME

Dear Addressee

The block style is easy to read. The date, inside address, salutation, paragraphs, and signature are all typed flush on the left margin.

The block letter may use open or standard (mixed) punctuation. This letter uses the open pattern.   Note that no punctuation follows the salutation or the complimentary close. For ease of reading all punctuation is kept to a minimum. Since this is a letter of medium length, the margins are one and a half inches on all sides. Extra blank lines are left between the dateline, inside address, and attention line to center the text on the page. The number of blank lines may vary between two to six lines depending on the length of the letter.

This letter also contains a complimentary close two lines under the final line of text. At least four lines are left for the signature. The secretary's initials and other end notes follow two lines below the signature block.

Complimentary close,

      (signature)

Signer's Name
Title

ini

Enclosure

MODIFIED BLOCK STYLE

COMPANY LETTERHEAD
Street
City, State ZIP

Month day, year

Addressee
Title
Company
Street
City, State ZIP

Dear Addressee:

The modified block style is a variation of block style. The chief difference is that the date is typed flush on the right margin and the complimentary close and signature block are also aligned on the right side of the page. The inside address, salutation, paragraph blocks, and end notation are typed flush on the left margin.

The modified block letter uses mixed punctuation. Thus, a colon appears at the end of the addressee's name in the salutation, and a comma is used after the complimentary close.

Spacing is also designed to give the letter a balanced look on the page. The secretary's initials appear two lines under the signature, followed by an enclosure note.

Complimentary close,

(signature)

Signer's Name, Title

Ini

Enclosure

SIMPLIFIED STYLE

COMPANY LETTERHEAD
Street
City, State ZIP

Month day year

Addressee
Title
Company
Street
City State ZIP

SUBJECT LINE

The simplified letter is another variation of block form. It was devised by the Administrative Management Society to simplify work for secretaries and to save time for readers. It uses open punctuation.

The simplified letter is typed in block format: dateline, inside address, paragraphs, signature block, and end notations are all typed flush on the left margin. A salutation and complimentary close are eliminated, and a subject line in capitals is substituted for the salutation. The subject line is separated by three blank lines from both the inside address and opening paragraph.

This letter is centered on the page. Since it is of medium length, three blank lines are left between the letterhead and dateline. The same space was left above the inside address. The signer's name and title appear in capitals. End notes follow block style form.

(signature)

SIGNER'S NAME, TITLE

ini

Encl.

MODIFIED SEMI-BLOCK STYLE

COMPANY LETTERHEAD
Street
City, State ZIP

Month day, year

Addressee
Title
Company
Street
City, State ZIP

Dear Addressee:

The modified semi-block letter is also an acceptable form. As does the modified block letter, it places the date and complimentary close on the right margin or near the center of the page. The inside address, salutation, paragraph blocks, and end notations appear on the left margin.

Note that the opening line of each paragraph is indented five to ten spaces. Standard (mixed) punctuation is most often used in this form. This letter is of moderate length, and the margins are set at one and a half inches. The complimentary close follows two lines after the final paragraph, and the secretary's initials are two lines beneath that.

The secretary should check to see the exact style preferred by the company before adopting this or any style.

Complimentary close,

(signature)

Signer's Name
Title

ini

Enclosures

INDENTED STYLE

Company Letterhead
Street
City, State ZIP

Month day, year.

Addressee,
    Company,
        Street,
            City, State,   ZIP.

Dear Addressee:

    The indented letter is not used in the United States, but it is still employed in Europe. The date appears on the right margin or near the center of the page. The first line of the inside address is flush on the left margin, but each subsequent line is indented five spaces. The first line of each paragraph is indented five to ten spaces.

    The indented letter uses closed punctuation.   Commas follow each line of the inside address, signature block, and end notations except the last line, which ends with a period.   No punctuation follows the secretary's initials.

    Again, this format does not appear in the United States, but it may be seen in foreign correspondence.

Complimentary close,

(signature)

Signer's Name,
Title.

ini

cc

SAMPLE BUSINESS LETTERS

Acknowledgment

Letters of acknowledgment verify a business transaction and indicate that your company is acting on it.

PURPOSE
1. To respond to an order
2. To advise of a shipment date or a service call
3. To thank a customer for a purchase, payment, or inquiry

FORM

Introduction
—refer specifically to the customer's request
—thank customer for interest

Body
—mention order number
—describe in detail the product or service
—include time and means of delivery

Conclusion
—express appreciation for business
—encourage further transactions

BURLAGE FURNITURE COMPANY
235 Arroyo Road
San Diego, CA 0000

May 27, 1994

Mr. Abed Darwish
Purchasing Agent
Phelps & Reese, Inc.
7671 Sullivan Drive
El Cajon, CA 00000

Dear Mr. Darwish:

We appreciate your purchase of Trendmaster Office Furniture from Burlage. We are sure that it will give your company many years of dependable and pleasurable use.

Delivery is scheduled by Carolina Freight for the morning of August 19. Your order (Invoice #B11654) includes three Model A32 Trendmaster Computer Desks with three Model C32 Comfortback Chairs. As you requested, the desks have a walnut finish, and the chairs are upholstered in tan naugehyde. Please inspect all merchandise upon delivery as Burlage Furniture cannot be responsible for damage in shipping. All Burlage merchandise carries a one-year guarantee against defects in design or manufacture.

Once again, we appreciate your confidence in our products. Please feel free to call me if you have any further questions.

Sincerely,

Eric Salvadori
Sales Manager

ES/lbr

Enclosures

Application

An application letter introduces the writer to a potential employer.

PURPOSE
1. To promote your qualifications for the job
2. To document your education and work experience
3. To arrange an interview
4. To persuade the reader to hire you

FORM

Introduction
—announce your intention to apply for the position
—state where you heard about the opening

Body
—document your qualifications
—list your relevant work and educational experience in logical order

Conclusion
—state your willingness to be interviewed
—thank reader for considering your application
—refer to resume or recommendations

73 Elm Street
Manassas, VA 00000
February 7, 1994

Ms. Francine Paliouras
Leesburg Real Estate
1406 Jones Street
Leesburg, Virginia 00000

Dear Ms. Paliouras:

I wish to apply for the position of receptionist and secretary that Leesburg Real Estate advertised in the <u>Leesburg Dispatch</u> on February 3. With an extensive background in a real-estate office I believe that I could be an asset to your company.

My education and work experience have given me excellent secretarial skills. After graduating from Stonewall Jackson High School in 1976, I enrolled in Lynch County Community College, where I received an associate's degree in secretarial science. I have mastery of several word-processing programs and am familiar with most spreadsheet packages. Since 1978 I have worked as a secretary and receptionist at Bull Run Realty. I have responsibility for all business correspondence from our office, including real-estate contracts.

I would be glad to meet with you for an interview. I can be reached at home after 5:00 on weekdays or all day on weekends; my phone number is 000-0000. Enclosed is my resume including references. I look forward to hearing from you.

Sincerely,

Keisha Powell

Follow-up (Job Application)

These letters acquaint a prospective employer with your persistent interest in an advertised position. One can be strategically sent at any stage of the application process, particularly if your initial letter has not been acknowledged. It may also be sent after an interview. Such a letter should link you to previous communications with the potential employer.

PURPOSE
   1. To remind the reader of your recent exchange
   2. To reiterate your interest in the position
   3. To keep your identity alive in the reader's mind

FORM

Introduction
—state date and nature of prior exchange

Body
—comment on continued interest in the position
—state your suitability for the position

Conclusion
—request permission to keep in touch
—express hope of a response

73 Elm Street
Manassas, VA 00000
March 1, 1994

Ms. Francine Paliouras
Leesburg Real Estate
1406 Jones Street
Leesburg, VA 00000

Dear Ms. Paliouras:

I sent you my resume and letter of application in answer to your advertisement for a receptionist and secretary in the February 3 <u>Leesburg Dispatch</u>.

Having worked for sixteen years in residential real-estate, I have the skills and experience to benefit Leesburg Real Estate. My present position is in a firm that is closing its home sales division.   I enjoy meeting potential home buyers and would like to continue working with a firm that specializes in residential properties. I know that Leesburg Real Estate has been a regional leader in this field.

I would very much appreciate learning if my application has reached you. I would be glad to submit further information about my qualifications. I may be reached at the above address, or feel free to call me at 000-0000.

Sincerely,

Keisha Powell

Appointments

An appointment letter details plans for a meeting or conference. For important engagements especially, a letter will verify the time, place, and date of the meeting.

PURPOSE
    1. To specify time and location of a meeting
    2. To confirm the appointment

FORM

Introduction
—detail date, time, and place

Body
—review reasons for the meeting
—discuss any preparations

Conclusion
—express pleasure about meeting

GEMMA INVESTMENT ASSOCIATES
111 EAST NINTH STREET, SUITE 23
NEW YORK, NEW YORK 00000

May 14, 1994

Mr. Chuang Chiu
Design Consultant
ASR Interiors
43 Madison Avenue
New York, NY 00000

Dear Chuang:

I want to confirm our luncheon appointment at Chez Lilah on Tuesday, May 27, at 12:30.

I have reviewed your preliminary drawings for our new offices, and they look well designed. You handled the enlarged reception area very well. Would it be possible for you to bring to the meeting an extra set of blueprints to pass along to our partners?

I am looking forward to the meeting. I believe we can resolve the few remaining problems then.

Best wishes,

Max Gemma

MG/bce

Appreciation

Letters of appreciation are a personal way to thank a person or a company for extraordinary help or cooperation, especially for donations to charity. They are also sent to customers to thank them for their business. A letter of appreciation may consist of a one- or two-paragraph note.

PURPOSE
   1. To encourage further efforts
   2. To acknowledge assistance
   3. To express thanks

FORM

Introduction
—state thanks
—set cordial tone

Body
—detail services or benefits available
—offer support to the reader

Conclusion
—express confidence
—seek to motivate the reader

Woodfin Foundation
17 Schoolhouse Road
Lima, Ohio 00000

December 27, 1994

Ms. Sylvia Turi
Keever Editorial Associates
33 Moby Road
Sandusky, Ohio 00000

Dear Ms. Turi:

On behalf of the Woodfin Foundation I wish to thank you and your staff for the extraordinary help in preparing our annual report. Your efforts are greatly appreciated.

The report looks splendid and has received much praise from our board. We apologize again for delivering the manuscript to you later than promised. Your staff performed beyond the call of duty in meeting the publication deadline for our annual meeting. Far from looking like a "rush job," the report looked very professional.

I just want you to know that the Woodfin Foundation appreciates your efforts--and we look forward to many years of continued business.

Sincerely,

Noah D. Aaron
President

tb

Collection (First Request)

The collection letter requests payment of money owed. The tone of a first request should be firm and persuasive, but friendly, to ensure the customer's cooperation and continued business.

PURPOSE
  1. To receive payment as quickly as possible
  2. To maintain the customer's goodwill

FORM

  Introduction
  —state desire for payment

  Body
  —describe in detail the nature of the debt
  —review previous notices of payment
  —suggest means of payment

  Conclusion
  —thank reader for action on payment
  —promote goodwill

ROVAL LUMBER COMPANY
455 Schuyler Avenue
Kearny, NJ 00000

November 19, 1994

Mr. Joshua Jonathan
Lake Lenore Construction
18 Maurice Boulevard
Denville, New Jersey 00000

Dear Mr. Jonathan:

We remind you that payment of your account at Roval Lumber is past due.

According to our records your account shows an outstanding debt of $484.32 for a casement window that was delivered on October 3 (Invoice #8364; your purchase order #7B88). We mailed you a collection notice on November 1, but have not yet received your payment. If you are not able to pay the balance in full at this time, please let us know and we will be glad to arrange an installment plan with you.

We greatly appreciate your immediate attention to this matter and anticipate hearing from you soon. Please disregard this notice if your check is in the mail.

Cordially,

Howard Boylan
Comptroller

Enclosures
   1. Invoice #8364 (copy)
   2. Credit statement

Collection (Subsequent Requests)

If an account is long overdue and reminders—either by letter or phone—have failed to secure payment, subsequent collection letters should be increasingly stronger and more demanding in tone. The letter may warn about possible legal action, repossession, the intervention of a collection agency, loss of credit rating, or garnisheeing of wages (where permitted). The letter may also note that the company is taking these actions reluctantly, having been forced to act by the customer's failure to fulfill his or her obligation.

PURPOSE
1. To demand immediate payment
2. To warn customer of negative consequences

FORM

Introduction
—state strongly the need for immediate payment
—emphasize creditor's responsibility

Body
—state amount of debt
—review history of collection efforts

Conclusion
—warn of negative consequences of inaction
—demand immediate payment

ROVAL LUMBER COMPANY
455 Schuyler Avenue
Kearny, NJ 00000

December 15, 1994

Mr. Joshua Jonathan
Lake Lenore Construction
18 Maurice Boulevard
Denville, New Jersey 00000

Dear Mr. Jonathan:

Your account at Roval Lumber is two months past due. If payment is not received immediately, we will have to take appropriate action.

Our records show an unpaid balance of $484.32. An installment payment was requested on November 19. Two notices have been sent since then. A minimum payment of $100 within five days will maintain your credit. We refer all our delinquent accounts to the Merchant's Credit Bureau.

We can continue to offer credit only if our customers meet their obligations. Please send your payment at once. Otherwise, Roval Lumber will have no choice but to turn over your account to the collection agency.

Sincerely,

Howard Boylan, Comptroller

Collection: First Notice (Preprinted)

This form letter serves as a first notice of a payment due. Blanks are left for the date, inside address, salutation, and such relevant data as the sum owed and the deadline. You may have a formatted notice in your computer program or you may use preprinted forms.

PURPOSE
1. To attract attention
2. To elicit payment of a past due account

FORM
Introduction
—note the sum due

Body
—request payment

Conclusion
—express thanks for the payment

CARPET UNIVERSE

811 San Pedro Road
Armadillo, Texas 00000

_____
(date)

_____

_____

_____
(inside address)

Dear _____:
(addressee)

Our credit department reports that your balance of   (amount)   is past due on
(date) .

We greatly appreciate your prompt payment of this sum. Thank you for your
attention to this matter.

Sincerely,

_____
Credit Manager

Collection Follow up (Preprinted)

Collection letters may use preprinted form letters. The letter may consist of a preprinted card enclosed in an envelope with a copy of the bill. Your computer program may include a preprinted form or allow you to create one.

PURPOSE
   1. To attract attention
   2. To elicit payment of an account past due

FORM

   Introduction
   —name creditor

   Body
   —state sum and date due

   Conclusion
   —list name of account, balance, and current date

CAROL ARTHUR FASHION
23 Jordan Street
Chicago, IL 00000

Dear Customer:

    Your balance is past due as of _____. We would appreciate immediate payment.

Account name: _____
Amount due: _____
Date: _____

CAROL ARTHUR FASHION
23 Jordan Street
Chicago, IL 00000

Dear Customer:

Your balance remains past due since _____, so we must again urge you to remit payment immediately.

Account name: _____
Amount due: _____
Date: _____

CAROL ARTHUR FASHION
23 Jordan Street
Chicago, IL 00000

Dear Customer:

We urgently request that you immediately pay your balance of _____, which has been outstanding since _____ despite multiple notices from us.

Account name: _____
Amount due: _____
Date: _____

Complaint

Complaint letters express dissatisfaction with a service or a product. Although the problem may arouse anger, a complaint letter should be firm, precise, and controlled in tone. The writer wants to persuade the reader to respond favorably by correcting the problem or by making an adjustment.

PURPOSE
 1. To inform the reader of an unsatisfactory service or
    product
 2. To receive compensation for the problem

FORM

Introduction
—identify the problem
—state reason for the complaint

Body
—give details about the product or service
—explain how you were inconvenienced
—request correction, compensation, or adjustment

Conclusion
—politely but firmly express thanks for action
—encourage goodwill

SHADYLAWN BAKERY 211 Shadylawn Road Elkton, DE 00000

March 23, 1994

DiMeo Truck Sales, Inc.
12 Franklin Street
Newark, DE 00000

Attention: Service Manager

Dear Sir or Madam:

On March 15 our delivery truck broke down three days after your service department had installed a rebuilt engine. It was then towed to your garage. Tony Czernowitz, your mechanic, rewired the generator and presented us with a bill for $105.00. He explained that the warranty covers parts only, not labor costs.

Shadylawn does not feel that these charges are justified. Poor service by DiMeo's mechanics, not our driver's negligence, was responsible for the truck's breakdown. We believe that DiMeo should stand behind its service and assume all costs of repairs.

Shadylawn has been satisfied with DiMeo Truck Sales over many years of business. We anticipate that you can resolve this problem so that we can maintain this relationship.

Sincerely,

Pat Sullivan
President

Congratulations

Congratulations are sent to a business contact to recognize promotions, awards, or special achievements. A letter of congratulations may be a one- or two-paragraph note; it can be handwritten if you wish to be very personal.

PURPOSE
1. To express admiration
2. To motivate through praise
3. To promote goodwill

FORM

Introduction
—state achievement
—set congratulatory tone

Body
—remark on appropriateness of recognition

Conclusion
—express personal pride in the accomplishment

CUTTER CREATIVE MANAGEMENT
SUITE 1501, TBA PLAZA
BOSTON, MA 00000

April 23, 1994

Peter Sacovich

CDK Advertising

16 Charles Street

Boston, MA 00000

Dear Pete:

I was delighted to read in <u>Advertising Today</u> that you've been awarded the Edgecomb Foundation's Silver Quill prize for ad copy. I've always thought that your work was the best in the industry, and I'm glad to see you get the recognition that you deserve.

Best,

Doug Hecht

acb

Credit Denied

A letter denying a request for credit preserves goodwill by maintaining a positive tone. It should be frank but tactful. Do not begin with the explicit refusal of credit, but suggest means to continue the customer's business.

PURPOSE
1. To inform the customer that purchases can only be made on a cash basis
2. To encourage the customer to continue business and to improve credit rating

FORM

Introduction
—review circumstances of credit request
—express thanks for customer's interest

Body
—state company policy on granting credit
—express regret at customer's current financial status

Conclusion
—suggest alternatives to credit buying
—invite further correspondence

PROCOM BUSINESS COMPUTERS/ 12 ELM STREET/ PHOENIX, AZ 0000

August 19, 1994

Ms. Elizabeth Perski
Sunburst Organic Grocers
21 Attermeier Drive
Tucson, AZ 00000

Dear Ms. Perski:

We are grateful for the promptness with which you supplied the financial statement we requested upon receiving your order (Invoice A-1678) for six Databank cash registers. Your determination to expand a small business in the current economic climate is commendable.

Our first step in considering applications for credit is to examine the applicant's bottom line for profitability after twenty-four consecutive months of business. As your venture is but six months old, we regret that we cannot at this time extend a line of credit.

We will be glad to do business with you on a cash basis for now, and will review your credit standing at the appropriate time. If your capitalization changes, please let us know. The Databank is the best register on the market for small business needs, and we promise you the best prices and services. We wish you luck with your enterprise and hope that we can be of future service to you.

Sincerely,

Jackson Knifechief,
Credit Manager

JK/as

Credit Granted

A letter granting credit should be affirmative, encouraging the customer to make purchases. The letter should be detailed, clearly stating the credit limit and the billing procedures. If the credit request accompanies an order, make note of its shipment.

PURPOSE
  1. To notify applicant of a line of credit
  2. To define the credit limit
  3. To describe purchase and billing procedures

FORM

  Introduction
  —express pleasure at applicant's financial status
  —state line of credit granted
  —note shipment of purchased goods (optional)

  Body
  —detail the credit arrangement
  —comment on benefits and limitations

  Conclusion
  —express optimism over ongoing relationship
  —invite more business

GOTHIC STAINED GLASS SUPPLIES
1313 WALPOLE ROAD
STRAWBERRY HILL, PA 00000

September 15, 1994

Ms. Carla Montoya
Valley Craft Stores
153 Hacienda Place
Houston, TX 00000

Dear Ms. Montoya:

We are pleased to inform you that your financial statement fully meets our standards of acceptability for a $10,000 line of credit, as you requested. The Luminous Lite stocked display case that you ordered pending the granting of credit has been shipped to you today by Leone Trucking. Your account has been billed for product cost and shipping charges of $2,726.32. An invoice is enclosed.

Gothic Glass now counts Valley Craft Stores among its valued customers. This means that you need only pay 50 percent of your bill upon receipt of your merchandise, with the balance payable at our regular terms of 1.5 percent 10 days, net 45. A smooth relationship over the next twenty-four months will double your credit line at that time, should you so desire. Regular customer status also guarantees that you will receive advance word of all sales and specials.

Thank you for your confidence in Gothic Glass. We pride ourselves on our quality products. Please feel free to call if you have any questions.

Sincerely,

Walt Hozak,
Credit Manager

Enclosures

      invoice #334A-2
      catalogue
      order forms

Credit Inquiry (Form Letter)

A company may use a form letter in response to an application for credit. It politely acknowledges the receipt of the order which accompanies the request, describes credit terms, and asks for a financial statement.

PURPOSE
1. To acknowledge the receipt of a customer's order and credit request
2. To request a financial statement
3. To establish a cordial relationship

FORM

Introduction
—acknowledge receipt of order and credit request
—express pleasure at beginning a new business relationship

Body
—describe credit terms
—request financial statement

Conclusion
—encourage more business

FONTANA FURNITURE
533 VENTURA BOULEVARD
LOS ANGELES, CA 00000

_____
(date)

_____
_____
_____
(inside address)

Dear_____:

Our shipping department has passed to us the credit request that accompanies your purchase order number _____, dated _____, for_____ _____. We are pleased to open your account and look forward to doing business with you.

Credit terms at Fontana Furniture are 10 percent on receipt of shipment, net 30 days. We are glad to open lines of credit with each customer whose financial statement passes our review. Would you please send or fax us your statement so that we can process it and proceed with your order?

Fontana Furniture appreciates your business, and please let us know how we can be of service to you.

Sincerely,

_____
Credit Office

Error: Mistake in Billing

This letter notifies a company that you have received a bill that contains an error. It should state the facts clearly and forthrightly, avoiding reprimands. A photocopy of the erroneous bill may be included. This letter may be as short as two or three sentences.

PURPOSE
1. To inform the correspondent of an error in billing
2. To detail the error and note correction

FORM

Introduction
—identify the bill

Body
—note the nature of the error

Conclusion
—stipulate the sum actually owed
—request a corrected invoice

THE GOLDEN WOK
133 Canal Street   New York, NY 00000

February 7, 1994

Pieter Vanderhoven
Consolidated Restaurant Supply.
115 East Fourteenth Street
New York, NY 00000

Dear Mr. Vanderhoven:

We have just received a Consolidated bill (No.677-211), dated January 30, 1994, in the amount of $123.50, for thirty place settings of Deluxe Baroque Flatware.

We believe this bill is in error. Please consult our purchase order number 342-C. We requested and were shipped the Standard model which lists for $93.50 in your catalogue, page 52.

The flatware we have received is entirely satisfactory. We will submit payment upon receipt of a corrected invoice.

Sincerely,

Ting Ho, Manager

encl

Error: Mistake in Payment

This letter notifies a customer that a mistake has been made in paying a bill. It should be tactful and courteous without admonishing the customer. The letter should describe the error and the means of correction and assure the reader of your company's goodwill.

PURPOSE
1. To note an error in payment
2. To request a correction of the problem

FORM

Introduction
—acknowledge the effort to pay

Body
—specify nature of error
—suggest means to rectify mistake

Conclusion
—assure reader of ongoing business relationship

FLORIDA FINANCIAL SERVICES
23 Federal Highway   Boca Raton FL 00000

April 23, 1994

Boulevard Management
3373 Pico Boulevard
Los Angeles, CA 00000

ATTENTION: Linda Gomez

Madam:

We are grateful for your prompt payment by check of our invoice #44522 in the amount of $11,750.00 for 100 shares of Promex Communication common stock.

We regret that a missing endorsement signature has caused our bank to refuse payment on your draft. Would you please either endorse the enclosed check or send us a new draft and return it to us by express mail?

We trust that this matter can be corrected promptly, and we look forward to future transactions.

Sincerely,

George Oxendine
Accountant Representative

hb

encl

Inquiry (Solicited)

Solicited letters of inquiry are written in response to either a personal request or a public advertisement. The solicitation may have come to you through a phone call, a newspaper advertisement, or an invitation to bid or submit a proposal, among others. The letter should recall to the reader the specific details of the solicitation. State the reasons why you are making an inquiry.

PURPOSE
   1. To acquire information
   2. To respond to the reader's request

FORM

Introduction
—recall the nature and date of the solicitation

Body
—describe specific situation or grounds of inquiry
—specify data needed

Conclusion
—state interest in further transactions
—express thanks for invitation to respond

FRANCONA ART / 21 Indian Blvd./Lewisburg, PA 00000

May 27, 1994

Mr. Frank Petraka
Executive Director
The Bloch Foundation
122 Valley Drive
Sunbury, PA 00000

Dear Mr. Petraka:

I received your letter dated 23 May requesting local artists to submit proposals for artwork in The Bloch Foundation headquarters currently under construction in Sunbury.

Francona Art represents twelve regional artists. We have exclusive rights to show and sell their works. We would be glad to meet with representatives of The Bloch Foundation to show you the range and depth of these artists. Their styles range from abstract to representational, and they work in a variety of media.

Please call our office directly at 000-0000, or fax your reply to 222-2222.

Sincerely,

Bruno Francona

ac

encl

Inquiry (Solicited, Follow up)

This letter is written to reinforce an unanswered letter of
solicitation. It seeks to obtain a response where the original letter failed. It should be cordial and specific, trying to
gain the reader's cooperation.

PURPOSE
1. To elicit a response from an unresponsive correspondent
2. To show that the writer is still interested

FORM

Introduction
—review the situation

Body
—suggest possible reasons for the absence of response
—supply more relevant data
—express hope that the response will be forthcoming

Conclusion
—emphasize mutual benefit
—express appreciation for reader's attention

FRANCONA ART / 21 Indian Blvd./Lewisburg, PA 00000

June 6, 1994

Mr. Frank Petraka
Executive Director
The Bloch Foundation
122 Valley Drive
Sunbury, PA 00000

Dear Mr. Petraka:

We wrote you two weeks ago in answer to your inquiry of 23 May soliciting artwork for your new headquarters building in Sunbury. Francona Art would be very interested in working with you.

We realize that your inquiry requested proposals directly from individual artists. Francona Art has exclusive rights to represent over a dozen local artists, and we cannot in fairness give favor to any one. We would be only too glad to have you visit our gallery, or, if you prefer, we could send you transparencies of our artists' works. At that point we would be glad to facilitate any arrangement between you and the artist.

We do hope to hear from you soon. We know that The Bloch Foundation has contributed generously to artistic and educational institutions in the Buffalo Valley. By purchasing works from Francona Art, the Foundation will help support local artists and provide a showcase for them.

We thank you for your consideration and look forward to hearing from you.

Sincerely,

Bruno Francona

et

Inquiry (Unsolicited)

Letters of inquiry are used by businesses to seek new customers, to test the market, or to obtain information. Frequently, businesses send unsolicited letters of inquiry as sales letters to potential customers.

PURPOSE
1. To obtain information on the price of goods or services
2. To start or continue a business relationship

FORM

Introduction
—state reason for inquiry

Body
—explain why the reader has been selected as subject of inquiry
—describe in detail the information requested

Conclusion
—extend thanks for the assistance

FREEHOLD LUBRICANT DISTRIBUTORS
213 AIRPORT ROAD   ALBANY, NY 00000

Yunis Auto Supply
2912 Highway 70 East
Troy, New York 00000

Dear Sir or Madam:

Subject: Discount Motor Oil

Freehold Lubricant Distributors is seeking retail outlets for its line of discount
motor oils, and we wish to inquire about your interest.

As one of the largest distributors in upstate New York, we can offer you exclusive
territorial rights to our product. Freehold's Highline Motor Oils are available in
quart containers in three popular weights, both detergent and non-detergent. They
are priced to sell about 10 percent below most major brands so that auto supply
stores and service stations can compete with the discount chains. We can also
package the oil with your logo and brand name, if you so desire.

Please contact our office, and we will arrange for a sales representative to call on
you. He will be glad to explain our terms, discount policies, and sales procedures.

Sincerely,

Richard O'Connor
President

DO/ss

Encl: Catalogue

Inquiry: Negative Answer

If the answer to an inquiry is "no," the letter of denial should still maintain a positive tone that shows sensitivity to the reader.

PURPOSE
1. To inform the reader that his or her request is denied
2. To encourage the reader's goodwill
3. To suggest means to correct the situation

FORM

Introduction
—establish rapport with reader

Body
—cite relevant information
—inform the reader politely that the answer is "no"

Conclusion
—try to suggest further possibilities
—give support to the reader

MONTROSS ALTERNATORS
311 Geth Avenue
Davis, CA 00000

October 16, 1994

Ms. Linda Calabria
34 Stackhouse Drive
Wallace, NC 00000

Dear Ms. Calabria:

I thank you for your phone call of October 14, and especially for informing us of potential wiring problems with the Model X alternator. Our production staff is now reinspecting all units, and we are reviewing our assembly procedures.

As you know, the alternator comes with a 90 day warranty for parts only. Montross stands fully behind our product, but we cannot honor obligations beyond these limits and still offer our unit at a competitive price. Therefore, I regret that we cannot reimburse you for labor costs as you have requested.

The Model X is an extremely dependable unit, and I am sure that it will offer you many years of reliable use. Please call me if you have any further questions about your alternator.

Cordially,

Derek Reese
Customer Relations

Inquiry: Positive Answer

Inquiries concern a wide variety of requests for information, products, or services. If the answer to an inquiry is "yes," maintain a positive and encouraging tone.

PURPOSE
1. To inform the reader of a positive answer to a request
2. To explain reasons for the decision

FORM

Introduction
—make a favorable response

Body
—explain relevant facts
—cite reasons for choice
—encourage more communication or business

Conclusion
—express goodwill
—offer further assistance

MANAGEMENT INSTITUTE OF AMERICA
233 Hidden Valley Road   Athens, GA   00000

March 12, 1994

Mr. Rashid Williams
Sullivan & McInnis
22 Salvadori Street
Jacksonville, FL 00000

Dear Mr. Williams:

We are pleased to accept your reservation to MIA's 1994 Executive Seminar. The Seminar will be held on June 5, at the Riverside Resort Hotel in Athens.

The 1994 Executive Seminar promises to be an outstanding program. The Saturday morning session will focus on "Climbing the Corporate Ladder" and will feature several well-known motivational speakers. The keynote address at the luncheon will be delivered by Dr. Frank Sura, the distinguished economist from the Free Enterprise Foundation. The afternoon program will feature a career-development panel titled "Tools of Trade," followed by small-group workshops. We will wrap up the Seminar with a cocktail party and banquet.

We thank you again for your interest in the Executive Seminar. Your place will be guaranteed upon receipt of the $750 registration fee which includes food, lodging, and airport transportation. We would appreciate your completing the enclosed forms. If you have any questions, please call me at 1-800-000-0000. Look forward to seeing you June 5!

Sincerely,

Brian Phelps
Administrative Director

Enclosures

Introduction

A letter of introduction attests to the financial integrity and good character of the person who bears it. It may be hand-delivered by the person described in the letter, faxed, or mailed prior to a meeting.

PURPOSE
1. To establish the personal, corporate, or financial integrity of the person described in the letter
2. To arrange the meeting of potential associates
3. To establish that the meeting would benefit all parties

FORM

Introduction
—present the person to the correspondent
—describe relationship to the writer

Body
—detail the person's qualifications
—state reasons to meet the person

Conclusion
—assert the personal or financial integrity of the person

FIRST NATIONAL BANK OF PITTSBORO
123 Main Street
Pittsboro, South Dakota 00000

October 6, 1994

Mr. Mohammed Said, Vice-President
Southeastern Bancorp
500 Bank Plaza
Atlanta, Georgia 00000

Dear Mr. Said:

I am writing to introduce you to Bill Schottstein, President of Fuchs Electronics and a member of our Board of Directors since 1983.

Mr. Schottstein and his firm have maintained an excellent credit rating with First National for 24 years. He will be in Atlanta on November 4 to attend the Consumer Electronics Convention. If he has need of banking services during his stay, the First National Bank of Pittsboro requests that every courtesy be extended to him. We vouch for his good character and financial integrity.

Please call me personally if you have any further questions or need to have his credit verified.

Sincerely,

First National Bank of Pittsboro

Bruce Peacock
President

BP/kt

Invitation (Accepting)

A letter of acceptance should be short and gracious. You may express gratitude for the invitation and express interest in the event. A one- or two-sentence note may be sufficient.

PURPOSE
1. To accept an invitation
2. To show appreciation

FORM

Introduction
—state that you accept

Body
—express interest
—repeat time and place

Conclusion
—thank reader for thoughtfulness

REGAL MOTOR FREIGHT   101 REGAL ROAD PARIS, TEXAS 00000

February 7, 1994

Mr. David Gila
Sales Agent
TOM Truck Sales
36 Haifa Drive
Canaan, Texas 00000

Dear Mr. Gila:

I've examined your sales literature and appreciate your invitation to take **a** closer look at the Mia truck line. Our firm is very interested in electric delivery vans, and I would like to see what you have to offer.

Thanks for the invitation, and I look forward to meeting you at The Towers on 21 February.

Sincerely,

Marilyn Peters
Vice President

Invitation (Declined)

This letter expresses the writer's regrets over an inability to accept an invitation. It should be succinct but polite. The writer may wish to offer an explanation. A few sentences should be adequate.

PURPOSE
1. To decline an invitation
2. To convey regret

FORM

Introduction
—acknowledge the invitation

Body
—comment on value of the invitation
—explain why it must be declined
—state regret

Conclusion
—express gratitude for invitation
—extend wishes for a successful event

REGAL MOTOR FREIGHT 101 REGAL ROAD PARIS, TEXAS 00000

February 7, 1994

Mr. David Gila
Sales Agent
TOM Truck Sales
36 Haifa Drive
Canaan, Texas 00000

Dear Dave:

I appreciate your sending me the literature on your electric delivery vans and inviting me to the presentation at The Towers on February 21. However, our firm does long-distance shipping exclusively, and we need trucks with capabilities well beyond the limited mileage range of electric delivery vans.

If we do decide to offer local delivery service, we will be sure to contact you. We wish you good luck with the Mia line and thank you for thinking of us

Sincerely,

Marilyn Peters
Vice President

qed

Invitation (Formal)

This letter extends an invitation on behalf of a person or a firm. It should be graceful, polite, and specific. The reader should be told why he or she has been invited, as well as where and when the event will be held. This letter may be as short as three sentences.

PURPOSES
1. To extend an invitation
2. To encourage the reader to accept

FORM

Introduction
—state time and place of the event
—invite the person or a representative of the firm

Body
—explain why the invitation has been extended

Conclusion
—express hope for a positive answer

TOM Truck Sales
36 Haifa Drive
Canaan, Texas 00000

February 3, 1994

Ms. Marilyn Peters, Vice President
Regal Motor Freight
101 French Road
Paris, Texas 00000

Dear Ms. Peters:

TOM Truck Sales invites you to an exclusive showing of the new Mia Electric Delivery Van. The presentation will take place at a luncheon at The Towers, 2100 Longhorn Boulevard, Houston, at 12:00 on February 21. We hope that you will be able to attend.

TOM Truck Sales is the sole regional sales agent for the Mia line. As you well know, recent technological advances have made electrically powered vehicles increasingly attractive to commercial users. The Mia offers reliability with superb economy, and it exceeds all state and federal environmental standards.

We are certain the Mia delivery van can improve your service—and your profits. We look forward to seeing you. Just call our office at 000-0000 and we will be glad to secure a place for you.

Sincerely,

TOM Transportation Services

David Gila, Sales Manager

Invitation (Informal)

An informal invitation is courteous and gracious, but brief. The letter should describe the occasion and express the host's wish to have the reader attend. The tone will be friendlier and more personal than that of a formal invitation.

PURPOSE
1. To invite the correspondent to an event
2. To motivate the person to attend

FORM

Introduction
—state where and when the event is to occur
—extend the invitation

Body
—describe the reason for the invitation

Closing
—express the hope that the person will attend

TOM Truck Sales
36 Haifa Drive
Canaan, Texas 00000

February 3, 1994

Ms. Marilyn Peters, Vice President
Regal Motor Freight
101 French Road
Paris, Texas 00000

Dear Marilyn,

We're giving a luncheon at The Towers at 12:00 on February 21 to introduce the Mia Electric Delivery Van. We're sure you'll find the presentation interesting.

As I mentioned to you at last week's Chamber of Commerce meeting, we have secured the regional franchise for the Mia line. The Mia represents a technological breakthrough. Its efficiency and low cost seem ideally suited for light freight handling.

We hope to see you on the twenty-first!

Best,

David Gila

Motivation

A letter of motivation encourages employees to increase their productivity.

PURPOSE
1. To praise an outstanding employee and encourage further excellence
2. To inspire an employee who is not performing up to standards

FORM

Introduction
—establish a positive tone
—find something to praise

Body
—show appreciation of accomplishments
—note obstacles to overcome
—suggest means to improve

Conclusion
—urge continued good work and effort

Piedmont Life and Casualty
701 Latta Road
Gretna, VA 00000

August 19, 1994

Karl Eckerman
211 Athens Street
Danville, VA 00000

Dear Karl:

This month marks the completion of your first year as our sales agent in Danville. We appreciate the long hours and hard work that you have dedicated to building a customer base there. You have an exemplary record, and the firm appreciates your efforts.

With the economic downturn of the past few months the entire insurance industry has been hurt. We hope that you will not feel discouraged if your first-year results did not meet your expectations. We feel assured that your efforts are building a foundation for future sales, and your commissions will climb accordingly. Business forecasts are sounding more optimistic, and we look forward to improved sales figures as the economy improves. The Southeast remains one of the fastest growing regions of the country.

Please know that Piedmont Life and Casualty appreciates how well you are representing us. We value you as an employee and look forward to productive years ahead.   Let us know if we can help you in any way.

Yours truly,

Jack McCloskey
Regional Sales Manager

Order

An order letter requests goods or services. "Please send" is the standard opening. Companies routinely use standard forms in place of letters. The order is often sent by fax.

PURPOSE
1. To place a written order for goods or services
2. To confirm in writing an order made by person or by telephone

FORM

Introduction
—state directly and in detail the goods or services requested

Body
—indicate relevant data as to quantity, size, color, or style
—cite identifying information such as serial number, catalogue page, or advertised source
—indicate unit price, subtotal cost, and total sum and method of payment
—include shipping information

Conclusion
—briefly thank the person or department for attentive service

GRECO HARDWARE 2113 Atlantic Avenue Brooklyn NY 00000

June 6, 1994

Catalogue Sales Department
Crown Supply
889 Hillary Parkway
Thomasville, NC 0000

Dear Sir or Madam:

Please send the following items listed in your Specialty Items Supplement, page 14, of your 1994 catalogue:

1 box (50 count)	TB1199 1" stainless steel cotter pins @$5.75		$5.75
2 boxes (25 count)	TB1207 2" stainless steel cotter pins @ 4.75		9.50
			$15.25

Please bill our account Number GH7771. Ship priority mail.

Thank you for your prompt service.

Sincerely,

Luis Pepe

Order: Follow up

If an order is not received or satisfactorily filled, a follow-up letter may be sent. The letter should refer by date and invoice number to the original order, describing the goods in detail. Specify what remedial action should be taken.

PURPOSE
1. To remind a supplier of an order
2. To motivate the supplier to fill the order or offer a satisfactory explanation

FORM

Introduction
—review history of the order

Body
—request the filling of the order
—explain reasons for urgency

Conclusion
—request refund or adjustment if order cannot be filled
—express confidence in supplier's good intentions

SENECA UNIVERSITY STUDENT STORES
BOX 112
SENECA, NY 00000

7 August 1994

Pathway Industries
333 Keever Drive
St. Louis, MO 00000

Dear Sir or Madam:

Subject: Invoice no. 10566-NC

On 25 May 1994, Student Stores ordered 1,000 ball-point pens with the University logo imprinted. The order included our check for $949.50 for cost and shipping. We anticipated delivery within 30 days.

We have not yet received shipment of the pens. We need them urgently to augment a public-relations campaign for the University's football team. If shipment cannot be arranged immediately, please inform us of the possible shipping date. If the order cannot be filled, please send a refund.

We appreciate your immediate attention.

Sincerely,

Toni Runningbear
Manager

ds

Order: Filled and Shipped (Form Letter)

This form letter confirms the receipt of an order and informs the customer of shipping arrangements. This letter may consist of a preprinted form kept on file in your computer. It may be sent by fax.

PURPOSE
  1. To acknowledge receipt of an order
  2. To note shipment of goods

FORM
  Introduction
  —state customer's invoice number, order date, description of goods

  Body
  —state date shipped

  Conclusion
  —express goodwill to customer

BOULDER CAMPING SUPPLIES
112 Rocky Road
Glenwood Springs, CO 00000

_____
(date)

_____

_____

_____
(inside address)

Dear _____:

Your order number _____, dated_____, for _____
_____, was received by us on _____.

Your merchandise was shipped on _____.

We appreciate your business.

Sincerely,

_____
Shipping agent

Order: Out of Stock (Form Letter)

This form letter is sent to customers when your firm is unable to fill an order because the item is out of stock. It should seek to maintain the customer's business and goodwill. This letter, too, may consist of a preprinted form and may be faxed to the customer.

PURPOSE
1. To inform a customer that the order cannot be filled immediately
2. To motivate the customer to wait

FORM

Introduction
—acknowledge receipt of the order

Body
—explain that goods are unavailable
—state date of anticipated shipment

Conclusion
—express regret at inconvenience
—encourage continued business

THE YARN BROKERS
65 Attermeier Drive
Milwaukee, WI 00000

_____
(date)

_____

_____

_____
(inside address)

Dear _____:

We received your order number _____ for _____
_____ on _____.

We regret that this order cannot be filled immediately, as we are temporarily out of stock. We anticipate shipping the merchandise to you by _____.

We regret any inconvenience this delay may have caused. We appreciate your business and look forward to serving you in the future.

Sincerely,

_____
Shipping

Political Action

Letters are frequently sent to government officials to support or oppose legislation or actions that affect a business directly or the business climate generally. The letter should be specific and build a strong factual case. Do not threaten, but you may remind the official of the consequences of his or her position. A courteous tone is most effective.

PURPOSE
1. To support or oppose a specific act
2. To convince the official to act in your behalf
3. To request assistance on a particular problem

FORM

Introduction
—cite the specific law or action
—state support or opposition

Body
—explain reasons for your stand
—cite facts and figures
—point to popular support for your position

Conclusion
—remind official of the consequences of his or her position
—thank official for considering your opinion
—ask for a response

RHODES TRAVEL SOUTH SQUARE MALL SANDUSKY OH 00000

2 March 1994

The Honorable Powell Ketchum
2345 Longworth HOB
Washington, DC 00000

Sir:

As president of Rhodes Travel, I urge you to oppose HR 3567 now being considered by the Ways and Means Committee. I believe the proposed excise tax on international airline tickets will seriously harm an already threatened industry.

Passenger loads have dropped almost 30 percent in the past twelve months, and a generally depressed economy has reduced international travel. Near-empty planes are commonplace. A surtax now would serve only to discourage travel. The airline industry has been troubled by increasing labor and fuel costs. Since deregulation, competition has lowered profit margins. The big three carriers reported record losses totaling $3.5 billion for the 1993 fiscal year. We need to create incentives for people to travel, not burden them with more penalties. HR 3567 is opposed not only by the travel industry and its professional associations, but also by labor and aircraft manufacturers.

The travel industry is a major employer which contributes billions in taxes and generates millions of jobs. We would hope that the government would support us rather than add to our problems.

It is in the best interest of the country for HR 3567 to be shelved. I look forward to hearing your position on this issue.

Sincerely,

Gus Mamoulian
President

Recommendation

A letter of recommendation offers an evaluation of an employee or colleague who is applying for another position. Your evaluation may determine whether the person is hired or not, so measure your words carefully. A person may be "highly recommended," "recommended," or "recommended with qualifications." This letter may be written generally to be kept on file or written specifically for a particular position.

PURPOSE
1. To provide personal and professional background on an employee or colleague
2. To evaluate the candidate's qualifications for another job

FORM

Introduction
—state the applicant's name and position applied for
—indicate briefly your recommendation

Body
—explain your relationship to the candidate
—define the applicant's strengths and weaknesses
—describe the person's abilities and accomplishments
—indicate the candidate's potential for growth

Conclusion
—summarize your evaluation
—urge reader to give applicant serious consideration
—offer to be available for further comment

PARKER INSURANCE AGENCY
112 Kupfer Boulevard
Brenda, OR 00000

July 23, 1994

Mr. Hatem Mansoor
Personnel Department
Ginsburg Department Stores
313 Cameron Avenue
Eugene, OR 00000

Dear Mr. Mansoor:

I am happy to recommend Wilsonia Peebles, who has applied for a sales position with Ginsburg Department Stores.

Ms. Peebles has worked under my supervision for three years as a receptionist and account secretary with our agency. She has maintained our files, handled billings, and kept records for several hundred accounts. I have always found her to be efficient, accurate, and honest.

Although she has not had experience with retail sales in our firm, we have found her to be pleasant and helpful when working with our customers. She has shown herself to be a quick learner who works well independently.

I will be sorry to lose Ms. Peebles, but I understand her desire to find a position closer to her home that can offer her more flexible hours. I think that you would be quite fortunate to have her on your staff, and I heartily recommend her.

Sincerely,

Linda Stuart
Office Manager

pc

Refund

A refund letter informs correspondents that you are crediting them for an overpayment for goods or services. Emphasize your company's reliability and promptness in correcting the problem. A corrected invoice may be included.

PURPOSE
1. To inform the customer of an error and state how refund will be made
2. To retain the customer's confidence

FORM

Introduction
—indicate amount of refund or correct cost

Body
—offer apology for any inconvenience
—indicate how the reimbursement is being paid or credited

Conclusion
—express appreciation for the customer's business
—offer to answer any questions

ENGLISH STATIONERS
5 Abbey Road
Dylan, OR 00000

7 February 1994

Mr. Shane Joyce
Michael Novelty Company
113 Wilmington Way
Lumberton, NC 00000

Dear Mr. Joyce:

Subject: Purchase Order 533-A

An audit of your account confirms that the correct cost of the business forms that you ordered on January 5, 1994, is $70.80.

Thank you for calling this matter to our attention. We apologize for any inconvenience this error has caused you. Your account has been amended to show a credit of $8.00, as requested in your letter of February 2.

A corrected invoice for $70.80 accompanies this letter. We value your business and look forward to serving you in the future. Please call me at 000-0000 if you have any questions.

Sincerely,

Thelma Arthur
Billing Department

unc

encl.

Request

A letter of request asks for information about products or services.

PURPOSE
1. To obtain information
2. To motivate reader to respond quickly and efficiently

FORM

Introduction
—make request for specific information

Body
—state your requirements as to rates, dates, or other needs

Conclusion
—express appreciation for rapid reply
—suggest possible benefits to the reader

WOLVERINE FINANCIAL SERVICES
311 Bank Street   Detroit, MI 00000

May 27, 1994

Laurel Hill Conference Center
36 Winding Hill Road
Laurel Hill, MI 00000

Dear Sir or Madam:

Could you please send us literature on the Laurel Hill Conference Center?   We would appreciate any material that illustrates the Center's facilities and its setting. Please also include a rate schedule.

We are in the preliminary stages of selecting a site for our annual staff retreat which will be held on a Saturday in April, 1995. We will need facilities that could accommodate 60 people for the one-day meeting. We would require at least three seminar rooms as well as catering facilities.

We hope to make a final selection of the site by July 1, so we would appreciate your prompt reply.   I would be glad to meet with your sales agent after reviewing your literature.

Sincerely,

Robert Sekora
Vice President

PN

Reservations

This letter makes or confirms a reservation for travel, facilities, or accommodations. It may be sent by fax.

PURPOSE
   1. To secure or confirm reservations
   2. To affirm length of stay
   3. To request special arrangements

FORM

Introduction
—state number in party and name on reservation
—specify type of accommodations
—specify length of stay

Body
—state arrival and departure times and dates
—explain special needs

Conclusion
—indicate amount and method of payment
—request written confirmation

THE JACKSON CLINIC
511 LAKE LENORE ROAD
JACKSON, MS 00000

March 19, 1994

Gateway Hotel
83 Palisades Avenue
San Diego, CA 00000

Dear Sir or Madam:

Please reserve a room for April 15 and 16 for Dr. Percy Walker, who will be attending the Society of Family Practitioners Convention.

Dr. Walker will arrive after 1:00 PM on Friday, April 15, and will be checking out after the final session on Sunday, April 17.   Dr. Walker would prefer a non-smoking room with a king-size bed.

We understand the convention rate is $129. Enclosed is a deposit for that amount for the first night. Full payment will be made with our corporate credit card. Please send us confirmation at your earliest convenience.

Sincerely,

Lisbeth O'Brien
Office Manager

Resignation

A letter of resignation should be firm and businesslike, whatever the cause of your quitting. State your determination to leave and briefly outline reasons. Acknowledge those who were helpful to you and express appreciation for the job. The reader may be called upon to recommend you when you apply for a new position.

PURPOSE
   1. To announce your intention to resign
   2. To explain reasons for quitting

FORM

   Introduction
   —declare that you are leaving
   —state effective date

   Body
   —briefly explain reasons for quitting
   —thank employer for cooperation

   Conclusion
   —express best wishes for future success

17-A Broadway Apartments
Durham, NH 00000
September 12, 1994

Mr. Harold LeBow
Smith & Guthridge
32 Ram Plaza
Greenville, NH 00000

Dear Mr. LeBow:

I wish to inform you that I will resign my position as sales agent as of January 1.

Having worked with Smith & Guthridge for four years, I have enjoyed my association with you and the staff. I have decided, however, to return to Boston to join the family business.

Working at Smith & Guthridge has been an important learning experience for me. I hope that I have contributed to the firm's success, and I wish you continued good fortune in the future.

Sincerely,

Irene McLeod

Season's Greetings

Season's greetings are sent to customers or associates to promote goodwill. Be as general as possible; for Christmas especially, be sensitive to the religious feelings of all your customers.

PURPOSE
1. To express holiday greetings
2. To thank customers for their loyalty

FORM

Introduction
—express holiday wishes

Body
—thank reader for loyal patronage

Conclusion
—extend personal greetings

OLYMPIA NATIONAL BANK
12 BRIDGE STREET OLYMPIC WA 00000

December 15, 1994

Mrs. Virginia Nettles-King
23 Woodside Lane
Fords, WA 00000

Dear Mrs. Nettles-King,

We at Olympia National Bank want to express to you our best wishes during this holiday season. We appreciate your patronage and look forward to serving you in the future.

May the new year bring you and your family health and happiness!

Yours truly

Walter Langmann
President

Sympathy

Letters of sympathy or condolence reflect close personal bonds. The salutation should reflect the degree of intimacy of the correspondent to the customer or staff member. A letter of sympathy may be a one- or two-paragraph note. It can be handwritten if the recipient is a close friend.

PURPOSE
   1. To express sympathy
   2. To offer aid or assistance

FORM

   Introduction
   —acknowledge the loss
   —set concerned tone

   Body
   —offer support

   Conclusion
   —express friendship
   —offer help

14 Saunders Road
Annapolis, MD 00000
October 30, 1994

Ms. Susan Barry
Chesapeake Investment Services
223 Kepley Road
Baltimore, MD 00000

Dear Susan,

    I have just learned from Donna Haley that your mother recently passed away.   I remember her as a very fine, warm person who always took an interest in the well being of others.

    We at Jordan Lake Enterprises want you to know that we're thinking of you. If we can help you in any way, please call upon us. We'd also like to contribute to a charity of your choice in her memory. Let us know what you think would be most appropriate.

                Best wishes,

                Jack Derrida

Transmittal

A letter of transmittal introduces a report to readers out-side of your company. Two or three sentences may be sufficient. A longer letter can offer a summary of the report, emphasizing its conclusions. (For another example of a letter of transmittal, see page 184.) Frequently, in-house reports will be accompanied by a memorandum of transmittal (see page 139).

PURPOSE
  1. To call attention to a formal report
  2. To emphasize the findings of the report
  3. To encourage reader's support and goodwill

FORM

Introduction
—describe subject of report
—state reasons for its distribution

Body
—summarize the report or its most important finding
—state your opinion of the report's value

Conclusion
—thank correspondent for reading the report
—ask for a response in writing, by telephone, or in personal consultation

PARKLAND CONSULTANTS
88 FREDONIA ROAD
JONESBORO, TN 00000

9 September 1994

Board of Commissioners
Franklin County
112 Main Street
Franklinton, TN 00000

Dear Commissioner:

We are pleased to submit to the Board of Commissioners the report on <u>Greenways in Franklin County</u>.

Our planning staff in consultation with the Citizens Advisory Board has studied the areas of concern requested by the Board in Resolution 3349, passed 12 January 1994. We considered the site selection of a Greenway in terms of its environmental impact, recreational opportunities, alternative transportation potential, and construction cost. We also studied state and federal regulations on funding and handicapped access.

Our recommendation is that Franklin County build a Greenway on the abandoned right of way of the Southeastern Railroad. We are confident that of the three alternatives this routing will best protect the environment and serve the interests of the citizens of Franklin County. Please call us at Parkland Consultants if you have any questions about any aspect of this study. We look forward to presenting this report to the Board of Commissioners at its 3 October meeting.

Yours truly,

Frank Lineberger
President

Enclosure: <u>Greenways in Franklin County</u>

Copies: LaVon Williams   William Rivers
         Blanche DuBose   Janice Lopes
         Theodore Capowski   Tommy Flaherty

Sales

The goal of sales letters is to be successful in winning sales of goods or services. Sales letters are of two basic types: the dramatic or "hard-sell" letter and the more restrained "soft-sell" letter. All good sales letters establish a friendly, conversational tone. They appeal to the emotions, but they also use testimonials, expert opinion, and independent test results to build a reasoned argument. Good sales letters anticipate objections and lead the reader through the sales presentation with rhetorical questions. The hard-sell letter differs from the soft-sell letter by tending toward emotional appeal and by exploiting graphics, type faces, and punctuation to emphasize the sales pitch. Word processing systems now allow mass mailings to be addressed —by name—to individual readers.

PURPOSE
1. To build direct sales business
2. To locate leads or encourage inquiries
3. To announce a new product and create a market
4. To secure new dealers or invigorate existing ones

FORM
Introduction
—capture reader's attention with a question, quotation, or dramatic statement
Body
—create a desire for the product or service
—convince the reader of its value
Conclusion
—encourage action for the sale
—make it convenient for the reader to buy or inquire further

SAFECO SECURITY SYSTEMS 11 Elm Road Peoria, IL 00000

Dear Mr. Savio:

Do you feel comfortable, Mr. Savio, reading about **house burglaries**
day after day in our local newspapers? Are you aware of the
statistics that show that the number of **house burglaries has
risen 74% in the past 5 years?** That criminals have **stolen an
estimated $750,000** from homes in the Peoria area alone in
the past 12 months?

Do you feel **secure** in your own home? Is your house **protected**
from the professional criminal? FBI statistics indicate that
across the country one **breaking and entering crime** is
reported, on the average, every 15 minutes, day and night.

Would a burglar find your house an inviting target? If you were a
burglar, would you break into a home knowing that it is hot
wired to the police? Or would you look elsewhere?

I think that you'll agree that knowing how to make your house more
secure is the best **protection** that you can give to your family
and possessions.

We at **SAFECO SECURITY SYSTEMS** would like to have one of our
Home Security Agents speak to you about how to make
your home **safe** from even the most experienced burglar.
The Agent will be glad to give your home a free security
inspection and leave with you, at no obligation, our **home
security** booklet, *Who Says Your House Is Safe?*

You'll learn
- what a master burglar looks for when he "cases a
joint"
- how he determines the best time to break in
- how he finds your hiding places for cash, jewelry,
and valuables
- HOW HE EVADES THOSE ALARM SYSTEMS YOU CAN
BUY AT YOUR LOCAL DISCOUNT STORE

SAFECO SECURITY SYSTEMS are the finest, most technologically
advanced units on the market. Our systems have been

endorsed by the National Association of Security Officers and the Consumer Safety Society. They meet or exceed all industry standards. For the past 23 years **SAFECO SECURITY SYSTEMS** have been **protecting** banks, factories, and retail stores across the Midwest.

SAFECO SECURITY SYSTEMS for the past three years has been making its **protective** devices available to you, the homeowner. We have already **protected** over 12,000 homes in the tri-state area. Your **SAFECO SECURITY SYSTEM** will be custom installed and periodically serviced for your full protection.

Now, thanks to breakthroughs in microelectronics, we can offer you a **SAFECO SECURITY SYSTEM** at rates far lower than you would expect to pay for **complete protection for your home.**

Can you, Mr. Savio, put a price on **peace of mind**?

Mail the enclosed card today. You'll get a free valuable booklet, *Who Says Your House is Safe?* And a **free security inspection** of your home. All you have to do is check **YES** on the enclosed card. Or telephone us at 000-0000.

Chris Mills
President, **Safeco Security Systems**

P. S. For your information we are including an article from <u>The Peoria Gazette </u>on how a **Safeco Security System** recently foiled a robbery attempt at a local residence.

SAFECO SECURITY SYSTEMS 11 Elm Road Peoria, IL 00000

December 27, 1994

Mr. Frank Savio
101 McRider Avenue
Peoria, IL 00000

Dear Mr. Savio:

We at Safeco Security Systems would like to acquaint you with a new product that we are offering to help you make your home more secure. For 23 years Safeco has been the leading commercial installer of security alarm systems. We are now offering that same protection to homeowners in the tri-state area.

You are no doubt aware of the dramatic rise in house burglaries in the Peoria area. Police statistics indicate a 74 percent rise in the past five years. The cost in the last 12 months alone is estimated at $750,000. According to the FBI, a breaking and entering is reported every 15 minutes, day and night, nationwide.

A Safeco Security System can be custom installed in your home at a price far below what you would expect to pay. Recent technological advances in microelectronics have made these units even more affordable. They come with an electronic alarm that will send a signal directly to your local police department or security patrol. In the past three years alone Safeco Security Systems has installed these home-protection devices in over 12,000 homes.

Safeco units comply with all state and federal regulations and meet or exceed all industry standards. Our systems have been endorsed by the National Association of Security Officers and the Consumer Safety Society.

Safeco Security Systems would be happy to have one of our Home Security Agents speak to you at no obligation. The Agent will be glad to give you a free home security inspection and leave for you, as a gift, a guidebook on protecting your house, <u>Home Safe Home</u>. Just check "yes" on the enclosed card or call our office at 000-0000 to arrange an appointment.

Sincerely,

Chris Mills
President

Business Letter Checklist

Letterhead or return address
Dateline
Confidential notation (optional)
Mail notation (optional)
Inside address
Attention line (optional)
Salutation
Subject Line (optional)
Introductory paragraph
Body paragraph(s)
Concluding paragraph
Complimentary close
Company name (optional)
Signature
Writer's name
Title or position (optional)
Identification initials (optional)
Enclosure notation (optional)
Carbon copy notation (optional)
Postscript (optional)
Mail notation (optional)

ENVELOPES

Addresses

Envelopes are addressed in block style. Businesses generally use envelopes with the company's name, address, and zip code preprinted in the upper left-hand corner. If the address is not preprinted or if the letter is personal, type the sender's name and address in the upper left-hand corner:

Mr. Thomas Hightower
112 Estes Street
San Antonio, TX 00000

The addressee's name should appear in the center of the envelope, so begin typing five to ten spaces left of center depending on the length of the name. The name, title, and address of the person receiving the letter should be the same as the inside address of the letter. The form should also be identical. Thus, if an attention line is used in the letter, it should also be included on the envelope. The two-letter Postal Service abbreviation should be used for the state. Several forms are acceptable:

Form	Sample
Name, Title	Mr. Gabriel Aaron, President
Organization	Kessler Records
Street	11 Noah Road
City, State ZIP	Dylan, MN 00000

Name	Mr. Gabriel Aaron
Title	President
Organization	Kessler Records
Department	Sales Division
Street	11 Noah Road
City, State ZIP	Dylan, MN 00000

Organization	Kessler Records
Department	Sales Division
Attention line	Attention: Gabriel Aaron
Street	11 Noah Road
City, State ZIP	Dylan, MN 00000

Name	Mr. Gabriel Aaron
In care of	In care of Frank Courtney
Street	11 Noah Road
City, State ZIP	Dylan, MN 00000

In cases of dual addresses—where a company may have both a street address and a box number—the postal service will deliver the letter to the lower address:

Name	Mr. Gabriel Aaron
Organization	Kessler Records
Building/Street	11 Noah Road
Box	Post Office Box 54
City, State ZIP	Dylan, MN 00000

Foreign Addresses

Styles vary in foreign countries. If possible, type a foreign address in the same form as the return address of the correspondence from abroad. The name of the country should appear in capitals by itself on the last line.

Special Instructions

If mailing or special instructions appear in the letter, they should also be typed on the envelope. Special messages for the reader—CONFIDENTIAL, IMMEDIATE ACTION, or PERSONAL—should be typed ten lines below the top in the left-hand corner. Special mailing instructions—AIR MAIL, SPECIAL DELIVERY, CERTIFIED, or REGISTERED—should be typed in capitals below the stamps.

Dr. Derek Hintoni $
33 Bailey Road
Pierre, SD 00000

CONFIDENTIAL   CERTIFIED MAIL

      Mr. Michael Joseph, President
      Wiener Marketing
      14 Rachel Boulevard
      San Antonio, TX 00000

Envelope Size

Business envelopes come in two popular sizes:

No. 6³/₄	3⁵/₈" X 6¹/₂"
No. 10	4¹/₈" X 9¹/₂"

Window Envelopes

When you use window envelopes, make sure that you center the address within the window so that the margin on each side is at least one quarter of an inch.

Postal Service Requirements

For machine processing, the U. S. Postal Service recommends typing the envelope address in capitals without punctuation:

MR GABRIEL AARON
KESSLER RECORDS
11 NOAH ROAD
DYLAN MN 00000

For optical scanning equipment, the Postal Service has set certain limits to the size of the envelope:

Height: $6^{1}/8$"
Length: $11^{1}/2$"
Thickness: $1/4$"

Both $6^{3}/4$ and No. 10 envelopes fit these requirements.

For optical character recognition, the address should fit within a box $2^{3}/8$" X 7". The margins should be at least 1" on the sides and $5/8$" on the bottom. For bar coding, the lower-right-hand corner should leave a $5/8$" X $4^{1}/4$" margin.

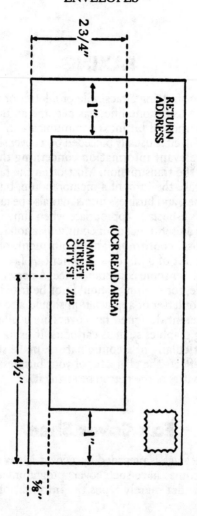

FAXING

Faxing, transmitting a facsimile of a letter or memorandum over a telephone line, has become an increasingly popular method of business communication. The correspondence itself is usually preceded by a cover sheet which contains relevant information concerning the circumstances of the transmission. Most often the fax message itself will take the form of a memorandum, but resumes, news releases, and business forms may also be faxed.

Faxing is especially appropriate when time is a critical factor. It is a useful means of communication for ordering merchandise, confirming an appointment, or acknowledging receipt of a bill or a shipment. A fax can be less appropriate for some correspondence. A personal letter of condolence, for example, should not be faxed. A formal invitation or letter of appreciation should also be mailed. Many different designed fax covers are available, some containing graphics such as cartoons. If using such a fax cover, particularly of a comic nature, make sure that it properly reflects the character of your business as well as the sensitivities of the person receiving it.

Fax Cover Sheet

The fax message is preceded by a cover. Many computers or fax machines have such covers programmed in them, and the sender merely types the information. The fax cover should include the receiver's name, the receiver's department and company, the receiver's fax number, the sender's name and company, the number of pages transmitted, and the date and time. Additionally, the sender may wish to communicate his or her own telephone number and return address. The fax cover may follow the form of a memorandum:

TO: Victor Rosenthal
Comptroller's Office
Torcelli & Berkowitz

FROM: George Gibbs

FAX NUMBER: 000/000-0000

RE: Board Meeting Agenda

DATE: 4/5/94

TIME: 2:15 PM

PAGES: 3

If you do not receive all pages,
please call 000/000-0000

THE MEMORANDUM

The memorandum, or memo, is used for written communications between offices or departments. Memos range from formal to informal, from one or two sentences to many pages. A memo may be a handwritten note to an employee confirming a meeting, a congratulatory notice to the company softball team, or an extended explanation of a company policy.

Generally, memos tend to be short and topical. They deal with routine company matters, serving as written reminders or announcements of important policies, events, and procedures. Memos are often used to confirm information that has been discussed in conversation, to record telephone messages, to make requests, to commend employees, to report information, or to transmit documents. Some firms use preprinted memo forms for routine correspondence outside the company—to order supplies or to confirm a delivery date, for example. Faxed communications frequently take the form of memos.

A memo, like all business correspondence, should be clear and concise. Make sure that the memo includes all relevant information as to time, place, date, order number, and so on. It is not necessary to add introductory or concluding remarks as in a business letter.

On some occasions, even for correspondence within an office, a letter may be more appropriate than a memo. A memo announcing the winner of a regional sales competition would be appropriate, but the employee should also be sent a personal letter of congratulations. Serious criticisms or censure of an employee should always come in a private letter, not in a public memo. A memo becomes part of the company's public record and any information of a private nature should be communicated through a phone call or personal meeting.

The Memorandum Form

Most firms use a standard form—either an off-the-shelf preprinted form or a company-designed form that may be programmed in a computer. This form may have preprinted lines or blank spaces after the guide words TO, FROM, DATE, and SUBJECT. Some firms use company letterhead stationery, sometimes on lesser-quality paper. For short communications the form is often note-sized (8$\frac{1}{2}$" X 5" or 4$\frac{1}{2}$" X 5$\frac{1}{2}$"). If your employer uses letterhead stationery for internal correspondence, you will need to type in the title MEMORANDUM and the guide words.

Parts of the Memorandum

Title

Indicate on the letterhead stationery that the correspondence is a memo by typing Memorandum flush on the left margin or centered three or more spaces beneath the letterhead. This title may also appear all in capitals and it may be underlined for emphasis:

MAX PLUMBING SUPPLY
16 Nicholas Street
Natchitoches, LA 00000

MEMORANDUM

MAX PLUMBING SUPPLY
16 Nicholas Street
Natchitoches, LA 00000

MEMORANDUM

To be less formal, you may use such titles as FROM THE DESK OF or INTEROFFICE MESSAGE in place of MEMORANDUM.

Receiver's Name

The receiver's name appears on the first line after the guide word *to*, and the salutation is omitted. Name alone is often sufficient, but especially in larger organizations, title and department or division may be included. Sometimes an address is helpful. Several forms, in either upper or lower case, are acceptable:

TO: Maria Hoza
To: Maria Hoza, Director
To: Maria Hoza, Director of Patient Accounts
TO: MARIA HOZA, DIRECTOR
PATIENT ACCOUNTS, 42 A WING

Frequently, memos are addressed to a group of employees, a department, or a division:

To: Patient Account Staff
TO: ALL EMPLOYEES

Sender's Name

The sender's name appears on the second line under the guide word *from*. Sometimes the sender will also be identified by title, position, or department, especially if the memo is a policy statement. To emphasize that the memo represents the company's views, not just those of the person sending it, the writer may omit his or her personal name and use only the division or department. Several styles are acceptable:

FROM: ROBERT GOLDBLATT
From: Robert Goldblatt, Director of Admissions
From: Director of Admissions
FROM THE ADMISSIONS DEPARTMENT

Date

The date is usually placed flush on the left margin under either *from* or *subject*. Three forms are acceptable for indicating the date of the memorandum:

traditional	Month day, year
August 19, 1994
government, science, military	day Month year
19 August 1994
informal, handwritten	month/day/year
8/19/94
European informal	day/month/year
19/8/94

If time is of critical importance, the time of day may also appear on this line. If time is not of any importance, the date may be omitted.

Subject Line

The subject line should make clear the purpose of the memo. The title or brief statement of the message's content should be as short and precise as possible. A glance at the subject line should instantly tell the person receiving the memo what the message concerns. It will also facilitate filing or placing the information on a calendar.

Avoid general titles such as "claims" or "employee relations." State the specific issue under consideration such as "health-insurance claims" or "new grievance guidelines."

The subject line is frequently capitalized. The Latin word *Re*, meaning "thing," may be used in place of "Subject":

SUBJECT: PARKING LOT ASSIGNMENTS
SUBJECT: Parking lot assignments
Subject: Parking lot assignments
RE: PARKING LOT ASSIGNMENTS
Re: Parking lot assignments

Brief memos with messages of temporary interest, such as report of a telephone call, may not include a subject line. For example, a short memo advising the recipient of a personal message from a spouse or confirming a doctor's appointment would not need a subject line.

Message Form

Most employers prefer left-margin block, but indented form may also be used. Check with your company to find the preferred style or follow the preprinted or programmed forms. While guidelines (TO, FROM, and so on) are usually double spaced, the message itself is single spaced, with double spacing between paragraphs.

Signature

Most memos are not signed, but the sender may place initials after his or her name in the FROM line. In longer or more formal memorandums, the FROM line is sometimes omitted, and the sender's identity (typed name and position and full signature) is placed at the end of the message.

Typist's Initials

Usually the initials of the typist are not included, but in longer memos they may be typed two spaces after the end of the message, in the same form as in a letter.

Enclosures and Copies

Copies and enclosures are included as end notes in the same form as they would be in a letter (see letter form, pages 19–20). Instead of listing copies, you may be asked to use preprinted memo forms which include ROUTING or a list of names. Each reader will sign his or her initials to acknowledge having read the memo and then pass it on to another person on the list.

Memorandum Typing Instructions

Letterhead
(3 spaces or more)

MEMORANDUM (centering and underlining optional)
(2 spaces)

TO: Name (title, division, or department optional)
(2 spaces)

FROM: Name (initials or signature optional)
(2 spaces)

DATE: Month day, year (time optional; placement optional)
(2 spaces)

SUBJECT: (or RE:) Brief title or statement of contents
(2 spaces or more)

The message itself is single spaced. Block style is preferred by most firms, but indented style may also be acceptable.

Double space between paragraphs. Keep paragraphs short.

(2 spaces)

(signature or typed name and title optional)
(2 spaces)

Typist's initials (optional)
(2 spaces)

Enclosures (optional)
(2 spaces)

Copies (optional)

SAMPLE MEMORANDUMS

Commendation or Congratulations

FROM THE DESK OF W. RUSSELL WEIL

TO: Ibrahim Saaed   DATE: December 27, 1994

On behalf of the firm, I want to offer my congratulations
on your election to the editorial board of *Modern Packaging
Design.* You've established yourself as one of the best
young designers, and we are proud of the national honor
conferred upon you. Thanks from all of us, and we really
appreciate all you've done in making Weil Manufacturing
an industry leader.

Company Policy

MOFFETT PUBLISHING
12 Chippewa Drive
Durham, NH 00000

MEMORANDUM

TO: All full-time, salaried employees

FROM: Arthur Hui, Chairman of the Board

SUBJECT: New health-insurance coverage

DATE: February 2, 1994

The Board of Directors of Moffett Publishing is pleased to announce that a new insurance policy offering comprehensive health coverage for all full-time, salaried employees and their immediate families will go into effect on April 1.

Transamerica Health will underwrite this much-improved policy. Representatives from Transamerica will be visiting us in March to explain the policy and to enroll employees and their families.

I am pleased that the Board has agreed to contract for this excellent coverage. We believe that this policy will ensure the economic viability of our company while giving our employees and their families the best protection possible.

(signature)

Company Policy Change

TRISTATE FINANCIAL SERVICES
SUITE 17, FRANKLIN PLAZA   LIMA, OH 00000

MEMORANDUM

To: Sales Staff

From: Tony Svoboda

Date: June 6, 1994

Re: PARKING FOR PERSONAL VEHICLES

As you know, construction of the new sales office is scheduled to begin this spring. During construction we will not be able to use our west parking lot. We have arranged to lease parking space for company vehicles at the Collestor Company lot across the street. Beginning March 15, however, those of you who drive to work will have to make other arrangements for parking your personal vehicles.

Limited on-street parking is available on Tigelman Street, or you may wish to use the municipal lot at Town Centre and walk the three blocks to the office. We will arrange morning and evening shuttle service from the office to this lot.

I apologize for the inconvenience, but I am sure that you will agree that the long-term benefits of the new facilities will greatly outweigh any temporary problems. When the construction is completed, we'll have a nicely landscaped parking lot with bright lighting and an assigned space for each staff member.

cc: Melinda Krehbiel   Mae Svensen
      Pat Suzuki   Kurt Summerfield
      Svan Chilkuri   Greg Pappas
      Deena Parisi   Bill Beckmann
      Hans Schwoerke   Maria Lopez

Inquiry

INTEROFFICE MESSAGE

TO: Kathy Ballenger, Inventory

FROM: Grady Kearns, Payroll

RE: Back order PY-77-71

DATE: 28 August 1994

On August 20 I asked the supply department to deliver three boxes of 3.5-inch disks (10 per box), inventory number C-14. I received a notice from you on August 21 that you were out of stock on this item but delivery was expected from OfficeMart on August 23.

Have you received this shipment? We urgently need the disks. If we do not have them in-house, I will need to make arrangements for a purchase order so that I can buy them from a local retail outlet. Please call me at extension 91.

Report (formal)

CITY OF GREENFIELD
TOWN HALL
PO BOX 112   GREENFIELD TN 00000

MEMORANDUM

TO: Members of the Appearance Commission

FROM: Department of City Planning

DATE: 12 March 1994

RE: Guidebook on the Greenfield Sign Ordinance

The Appearance Commission has asked this office for suggestions on improving enforcement of the Greenfield Sign Ordinance, enacted by the Town Council on 14 December 1994.

<u>Problem</u>: The Appearance Commission is charged with protecting the character of Greenfield as a historic village. The Commission has attempted to balance the need for retail businesses to advertise their services and products with the concern of local residents that Greenfield retain its traditional character. Greenfield's special ambiance as a historic village makes the town a pleasant place to live and draws tourists to the area. The newly enacted Sign Ordinance attempts to regulate the appearance of commercial signs in the village, both setting guidelines for new signs and calling for the removal or renovation of some existing signs. The Commission is concerned about enforcing this ordinance fairly and impartially. Several businesses have already complained to the Commissioners and Town Council about the potential effects of the ordinance.

<u>Areas of Concern</u>: On 8 March, the Appearance Commission met with an ad hoc committee of the Chamber of Commerce. Several areas of concern in interpreting and enforcing the new ordinance were defined:

 •Size of sign
 •Location
 •Materials
 •Colors
 •Lighting
 •Three-dimensional figures and graphics

•Coordination in size and design with architecture
•Logos and franchise signs

<u>Recommendations</u>: The Appearance Commission recommends the publication by 1 August 1994 of a Commercial Sign Guidebook listing specific criteria for designing new signs and renovating existing ones.

In April the Commission should schedule public meetings to explain the ordinance and to hear public opinion. Representatives of the business community, such as the Chamber of Commerce, and citizens groups, such as the Greenfield Preservation Society, should be invited to participate.

Based on public comment, the Commission will pass its recommendations to the Town Council dealing with aspects of the Ordinance that are ambiguous or subject to interpretation. There is presently no regulation, for example, of portable signs. Other signs that do not conform to the Ordinance may be deemed to have "historic" worth by virtue of their longevity or aesthetic merits. Drafting a guidebook should help the Commissioners formulate policy that would cover such cases.

After the April hearings, the Commission will draw a list of recommendations. A draft of a Commercial Sign Guidebook will be submitted to the Town Council, local businesses, and community representatives for their comments. At this point the Town Council may wish to add amendments to the Ordinance to correct any ambiguities or omissions. A revised handbook would then be published.

This office will be glad to meet with the Appearance Commission at any time to begin the process of drafting a Commercial Sign Guidebook. We are prepared to offer legal and professional counsel as well as secretarial assistance.

Frank Thompson
Director, Department of City Planning

Report (informal)

RANCHERO ESTATES
12 Hacienda Trail   Los Alamos, NM 00000

MEMORANDUM

To: Sales Agents

From: Frank Gonzalez, President

Date: 2 March 1994

Subject: February Housing Sales UP!

The stats are in for housing sales in February and the market looks to be strengthening. We sold 121 units a 20% increase from last month and 33% higher than the figures for February 1993. Much of the improvement comes from new people moving into the area for the Formax Corporation plant which will begin production on 15 March. Interest rates in February remained at just above 7% which also helped spur sales. The prospect is for these rates to climb gradually in the coming months, so agents may wish to stress to customers the advantages of making their purchases now. At the staff meeting on 10 March we will present a more complete report on sales, but the preliminary data suggest that the market is still strongest for starter homes under $125,000 and weakest at price levels above $250,000.

Scheduling a Meeting

TO: STUDENT AFFAIRS STAFF

FROM: MIMI GRIMES

SUBJECT: JULY STAFF MEETING

Please mark your calendars and plan to attend the monthly staff meeting, Monday, July 24, at 3:00 in the conference room, 103 Peabody Hall.

Transmitting Documents

MEMORANDUM

TO: Tanya Potter
            Ramiah Sarik
            Bill McGuire
            Emily Ann Fucello

FROM: Rachel Strauss

DATE: MARCH 15, 1994

RE: FISCAL 1993 OPERATIONS ENERGY AUDIT

O'Brien and Levin have completed their energy audit of our Westminster plant. I am sending a copy of their report with this memo. It is the most comprehensive analysis that I have seen to date of the plant's operations. I call special attention to their recommendations.

Please read the report closely, and let me know as soon as possible what steps that you think we should take to improve operating efficiency. It would be helpful if you would send me your recommendations to review before we meet. Once we achieve a consensus on a plan of action we should arrange a conference with senior management.

Memorandum Checklist

Title (Memorandum or Interoffice Message)
To
From
Date (placement optional)
Subject or Re
Message
Signature or initials (optional)
Typist's initials (optional)
Enclosures (optional)
Copies or routing (optional)

MINUTES

Minutes are a written record of the transactions and recommendations of a meeting. They are usually taken by a secretary or committee member. The minutes are filed as a permanent record of the meeting. Copies are passed to the participants and other interested parties prior to their reconvening. Minutes must be clear, precise, and accurate.

When taking minutes, be sure to bring sufficient pens and note-taking paper. Your company may also want you to record the meeting with dictation equipment. The minutes should contain only major topics and recommendations, not every point that was discussed. Since some speakers may not stick to the subject, you may have to rearrange the material when preparing the minutes. Keep your handwritten notes on file for verification. The typed minutes are an organized and condensed version of the meeting. The tone should be formal and objective, reporting the major points and the names of the persons making them.

After the minutes are completed, they are usually first passed to the chairman or president for approval and then circulated to the participants as well as to absent members. The minutes should be submitted as soon as possible and distributed prior to the next meeting of the group. At the next meeting each member will have a copy of the minutes; as a first order of business, the minutes will be amended or corrected, and approved by vote. The secretary then signs the minutes with the notation, *approved*.

Each organization follows a house style in minutes. Informal minutes may be a simple chronological summary of what transpired in the meeting. For legal or organizational reasons the minutes may be typed as a formal report, reflecting an agenda or a prearranged plan. Importantly, the minutes should follow a uniform format meeting after meeting.

Parts of Minutes

Title

Several styles are acceptable. A topic heading is direct and easy to read. Type "Minutes" either at the left margin or center of the page. The name of the committee or organization, the type of meeting, date, and place may follow it:

Minutes: Wordsworth Literary Society, Monthly Meeting, November 23, 1994

Or you may begin with a complete sentence conveying information as to the reason for the meeting, the name of the group, the date and place of the meeting:

The annual meeting of Friends of Northwood Hospice was held on August 3, 1994, in the board room of Riverdale Hospital, Farmingdale, NY.

Attendance

The minutes should list the names of those who attended
the meeting beginning with the presiding officer.

> Present: Sol Terry Reaper, chair; Lucinda
> McAdams, Julie Mendoza, Su Ling, and
> Angela Suarez
> Chairperson Lillian Goldblum presided with
> forty-two members in attendance.
> President Steven Valente welcomed ninety-seven
> delegates to the plenary session.

Approval of Minutes

A short statement should be made noting any corrections
or amendments to the reading of the minutes of the previous meeting. The name of the person making the
motion for approval of the minutes should be stated:

> William Stetson moved that the minutes be
> approved. The motion was seconded and
> carried.

Report

The text can take several forms. Informal minutes will
just summarize chronologically the major points discussed at the meeting. Formal minutes will break down
the discussion into subtopics based on the meeting's

agenda, oral reports, or subjects discussed. The headings, placed against the left margin, may be underlined, bold-faced, or italicized for emphasis:

Treasurer's Report
<u>Treasurer's</u> <u>Report</u>
Treasurer's Report

After all agenda matters have been covered and all reports presented, space will be reserved for Unfinished Business or New Business.

Date of Next Meeting

A statement of the time and place of the next meeting may be placed at the end of the report or at the beginning (after the attendance). This information may be capital-ized to capture the reader's attention.

> NEXT MEETING: 7:30 PM, JANUARY 4, 1992,
> AT BOARD ROOM, VALLEY NATIONAL
> BANK, WAYNE, NJ

Sample Minutes (informal)

A monthly meeting of the Ditto Industries Employee Social Welfare Committee was held at 2:00 PM, April 15, 1994, in Suite 15 of the Administration Building. Attending were Joe Ciao (chair), Ezell Jackson, Loretta Sanchez, Malik Stapleton, and Regina Johnston.

The Committee agreed that we would once again hold a company fundraiser for the Fairview Children's Hospital. Ezell pointed out that last year's campaign, a sale of chocolates, was disappointing. He reported that we only raised $440 for the hospital on sales of $940, and less than half of the employees participated. Regina and Loretta pointed out that selling chocolates may be a poor choice at a time when people seem so diet conscious. We decided to explore new possibilities. Some members suggested that we find a product that would have more sales appeal and would yield higher profits. Suggestions included stationery, coffee mugs, or t-shirts. Others spoke in support of holding a company fundraising event like a picnic or softball game. Loretta and Malik agreed to study the alternatives and report back at the next meeting. Joe said he would compile a new list of fundraising captains in each department. He also suggested that we set a minimal fundraising goal of $1,000 this year.

The meeting adjourned at 2:50 PM.

THE NEXT MEETING WILL BE HELD 2:00 PM, MAY 14, IN SUITE 15, ADMINISTRATION BUILDING

Loretta Sanchez, Secretary

Sample Minutes (formal)

Minutes: Pottstown Parks Citizens Advisory Committee, July 1, 1994, at Town Council Chambers

Present: Terri Malovich, chairperson; Francine Stella, secretary; Boyd Benson, Henry Krizek, Gregory Christakos, John Ocharenko, Janet Miller, Rudolph Perkins, Stanley Kowalski, Ryan Flaherty, Julian Cohen, and Steve Petrus. Also present was Bill Clay, assistant manager of the Pottstown Parks Department.

Approval of the Minutes

Upon reading of the June 3 minutes Boyd Benson observed that his name had been omitted from those in attendance. The minutes were so amended. Julian Cohen moved that the minutes be approved. The motion was seconded and carried.

Greenwood Park Expansion

Bill Clay of the Pottstown Parks Department reported that the Town Council had authorized the purchase of 12 acres to expand Greenwood Park. The Council wants the Citizens Advisory Committee to recommend possible uses for this land. The Parks Department defined several alternatives:

> Natural environment area
> Recreational fields
> Mixed use

Gregory Christakos spoke in favor of keeping the area natural, noting that the site includes extensive woodlands and streams which would make it ideal for trails and rustic picnic areas. John Ocharenko pointed out that the town park system lacks undeveloped land where people can "commune with nature." He also pointed out the need for environmental protection. Francine Stella noted that current recreational facilities are overtaxed, and the youth soccer league has had to turn down applicants because of the lack of playing fields. Chair Terri Malovich suggested the possibility of a mixed-use compromise and requested volunteers for a subcommittee to explore the issue. Francine Stella, John Ocharenko, Julian Cohen, and Janet Miller agreed to serve.

Pottstown Street Fair

Terri Malovich noted that the Pottstown Street Fair will be held on Saturday, June 1, and she recommended that the Citizens Advisory Committee again set up a booth. We would distribute literature, erect displays, and have volunteers available to answer questions. Boyd Benson moved that the chair be authorized to appropriate $50 for a Street Fair booth. The motion was seconded and carried without debate.

Unfinished Business

Ryan Flaherty stated that he has been trying to find new members to join the Committee, but has nothing definite to report. Several people mentioned that they are "interested" but have not yet committed.

New Business

Steve Petrus reported that he has received numerous complaints that the $25 enrollment fee for participation in the Pottstown Summer Softball League is excessive. He noted that the fee was especially hard for families who had several members participating. Henry Krizek moved that we ask the Parks Department to send a representative to our August meeting to explain the rates. The motion was seconded and carried.

The meeting adjourned at 10:00 PM.

NEXT MEETING: 7:30 PM, AUGUST 2, 1994, AT THE TOWN COUNCIL CHAMBERS, MAIN STREET

> Francine Stella
> Secretary

Minutes Checklist

Organization name
Time, date, place of meeting
Attendees beginning with chair
Approval of past minutes
Agenda topics or reports
Unfinished business
New business
Adjournment time
Date of next meeting (placement optional)
Approval and secretary's signature

NEWS RELEASE

A firm seeks to promote its services or products through attention-getting news releases. A news release should describe an event of significance: a new product or service, opening a business, a new branch or location, major expansion, reorganization, or new management. The release should be vivid, clear, and specific, written in journalistic style. The information is presented from most important to least important, from main ideas to specific facts. It begins by answering who, what, when, where, why, and how.

The style and tone should be clear and easy to read. Do not exaggerate the importance of the event through "hard sell" or excessive superlatives. Photos may be appended by paper clip, not by glue or staples. Cover letters other than follow ups are not necessary. The data must be current. Remember that an editor may choose to print only part of your release, often only the first sentence. Make every word count.

Parts of a News Release

Title

Center NEWS RELEASE or PRESS RELEASE in capitals on the center of the page.

Heading

The news release begins with information for the newspaper editor. Two lines below the title, type in the heading flush with the left margin. The heading includes the name of the company, the contact person for the release, the contact person's telephone number and company address, and the release date. (FOR IMMEDIATE RELEASE or FOR RELEASE ON DECEMBER 27, 1994.)

SHADY KENNELS, INC.
contact: Gracie Crowther
telephone: 000-000-0000
118 Homer Road
Jaffa, KY 00000
FOR RELEASE ON FEBRUARY 2, 1994

Subject Line

Two lines below the heading, center the subject line in capitals. The title should convey the company's business and the subject of the release.

GRAND OPENING OF SHAGGY DOG
BOARDING KENNELS

Dateline

Two lines below the subject line, indent two spaces and enter the dateline, composed of the city (and, if necessary, the state) and the date in upper and lower case, followed by a dash.

Jaffa, KY, February 2, 1994—
Chicago, May 14, 1994—

The text follows immediately after the dash.

Typing Instructions

The news release should be double-spaced with one-inch margins. Use 8½" X 11" paper. The release should be on a single sheet, if possible. If more than one page is required, center the word MORE in capitals at the bottom of the page and begin the next page flush on the margin with a one-word title and page number:

Kennels-2

At the end of the news release, center one of the following:

###
(END)

Sample News Release

NEWS RELEASE

COMET DRUGS
contact: Abdul Khalid
telephone: 000-000-00000
123 Garner Lane
Hartford, CT 00000
FOR IMMEDIATE RELEASE

ARI BOYAN NEW PRESIDENT OF COMET DRUGS

Hartford, CT, April 24, 1994 — Comet Drugs, the Hartford-based discount drugstore chain, has announced the appointment of Ari Boyan as president, effective May 1.

"Boyan brings to Comet Drugs broad experience as a retail manager with special expertise in the pharmaceutical field," stated Harold Kaplan, board chairman. For the past seven years Boyan has served as executive vice president of Z-Mart Department Stores where he was responsible for establishing full-service pharmacies in the national discount chain. Boyan, 43, holds a B.S. in pharmacology from the University of North Carolina and a M.B.A. from Duke University. "I remain committed to Comet's policy of offering high-quality generic products at competitive prices," Boyan stated at a press conference announcing his appointment.

Since its founding in Hartford in 1978, Comet has grown rapidly to become one of New England's leading retail drugstore chains. It now operates 124 stores in a five-state area. Its gross sales were $259 million in 1994.

###

RESUME

The resume is a personal data sheet which accompanies a letter of application for a job. The resume may be filed with a placement service or employment agency. It should be clean, orderly, and attractive as it represents the applicant's character and qualifications. Word processing and desktop publishing allow you to design a resume with a variety of fonts and layouts. You can readily tailor the contents for a specific position, emphasizing those aspects of your education or work experience that are most relevant. A good resume can win an applicant an interview.

Resumes come in a variety of formats. The resume should be tailored to meet the specific requirements for the job desired. Professional people often are asked to file a form of the resume called a vita—a Latin word meaning "life"—when applying for grants or other technical work. The vita includes sections on research and publication. Some resumes include past job descriptions, listing responsibilities and special skills. The two basic forms of the resume, however, are the chronological and the functional.

Chronological Resume

The chronological resume is organized by time. It presents general information, so it can be used for a variety of purposes, not just for a specific position. It is designed to present the applicant's background clearly and easily so that

an employer can review quickly the person's qualifications.
(For this reason, try to fit your resume on one page.) The
chronological resume is especially appropriate for recent
graduates or persons with minimal work experience.

Functional Resume

The functional resume is organized by categories that are
relevant to a specific job. These categories may include
career goals, work experience, or special skills. It high-
lights areas that would appeal to a particular employer.
Though done in outline form, the functional resume may
use paragraph blocks. Under each section, phrases rather
than sentences are acceptable.

Parts of the Resume

Personal Data

The resume—whether chronological or functional—
should list your name, address, and telephone number at
the top.

Tyrone Curtis Stephens
22 Elm Street
Houston, Texas 00000
(111) 222-3333

Career Objective

A resume can state your ultimate goal or specific job interest in seeking employment. The chronological resume usually consists of a short general statement while the functional resume may be more specific.

(chronological)

CAREER GOAL   Retail sales management

(functional)

Career Objective

Seeking position as manager at a retail department store or franchise outlet. Special interest in athletic gear and sporting goods.

Education

List your educational record from present to past. You may also add your degrees, major areas of study, and special honors.

(chronological)

EDUCATION

> 1991-1992: B.S., Wayne State University
> Major: Business Administration
> 1990-1991: A.S., Vincennes Junior College
> Major: Business

(functional)

Educational Background in Business

Received a Bachelor of Science from Wayne State University in 1992; majored in business administration, concentrating on marketing and management. Received an A.S. in 1991 from Vincennes Junior College in business with on-job training in retail sales.

Employment History

List your work experience beginning with your most recent job and going back to your graduation from high school or college. Again, several formats are acceptable. The information should reflect those qualifications that you wish to emphasize. In the chronological resume give enough data so that the person reviewing your resume could locate your employers. Do not leave gaps in time.

(chronological)

WORK EXPERIENCE

    1992-1994: Assistant Manager, Mercury Sporting
               Goods, Livonia, MI
    1991-1992: Sales Associate, Footfast Athletic Shoes,
               Vincennes, IN
    1989-1991: Salesman, Bullard's Discount Sales, Gary,
               IN

(functional)

Retail Sales Manager

Broad retail sales experience in customer service and management. Two years as Assistant Manager of Mercury Sporting Goods, Livonia, MI with responsibility for scheduling, stocking, and accounting. Sales Associate at Footfast Athletic Shoes, Vincennes, IN, working in direct sales, familiarity with sports shoes products and market demand. Salesman at Bullard's Discount Sales, Gary, IN, responsible for stocking and customer relations.

Activities

This section should list activities, awards, interests, hobbies, or memberships that you believe would appeal to a prospective employer. If you are applying for a newspaper job, for example, you might wish to list publications, school honors, or special talents.

(general)

Activities and Interests

    Volunteer Work: YMCA Basketball Coach, Big
                    Brother, Fellowship of Christian
                    Athletes
    Hobbies: track, basketball, photography
    Honors: YMCA Coach of the Year; FCA, chapter
             president

(functional)

Community Service

   Have worked as a volunteer with youth sports team. Served as Big Brother to inner-city, grammar-school child. Volunteered as YMCA Basketball coach, voted coach of the year. Elected president of collegiate Fellowship of Christian Athletes chapter.

References

You may merely state that references are available upon request at the left margin or centered at the bottom of your resume. Be sure that you have the permission of your references before using their names.

(general)

References are available upon request.

Sample Chronological Resume

PERSONAL	Tyrone Curtis Stephens 12 Elm Street Houston, Texas 00000 (111) 222-3333
EDUCATION	1991-1992: B.S., Wayne State University, Detroit, MI Major: Business Administration 1990-1991: A.S., Vincennes Junior College, Vincennes, IN Major: Business
EMPLOYMENT	1992-1994: Assistant Manager, Mercury Sporting Goods, Livonia, MI 1991-1992: Sales Associate, Footfast Athletic Shoes, Vincennes, IN 1989-1991: Salesman, Bullard's Sales, Gary, IN 00000
COMMUNITY SERVICE	1991-1994 YMCA Basketball Coach, Detroit, MI 1990-1991 Big Brother volunteer, Gary, IN 1992-1994 Fellowship of Christian Athletes
HONORS	Basketball scholarship, Vincennes Junior College Coach of the Year, Detroit YMCA Fellowship of Christian Athletes, chapter president
REFERENCES	Available upon request

Sample Functional Resume

Tyrone Curtis Stephens
22 Elm Street
Houston, Texas 00000
(000) 111-222-333

**Career
Objectives**   My goal is to work for a retail firm specializing in direct customer sales of sporting goods. I have experience in this field and am seeking an entry-level managerial position in a franchise or department store.

Education   Received a B.S. in Business Administration from Wayne State University in 1992 with a concentration in marketing and management. Earned an A.S. in Business from Vincennes Junior College where I participated in a work-study program.

**Retail Sales
Experience**   Broad experience in retail sales both in customer service and management. Two years as Assistant Manager of Mercury Sporting Goods, Livonia, MI, with responsibility for scheduling, stocking, and accounting. Sales Associate at Footfast Athletic Shoes, Vincennes, IN, working in direct sales, familiarity with sports shoes products and market demand. Salesman at Bullard's Discount Sales, Gary, IN, responsible for stocking and customer relations.

**Community
Service**   Have worked as a volunteer with youth sports team. Served as Big Brother to inner-city, grammar-school child. Volunteered as YMCA Basketball coach, voted coach of the year. Elected president of collegiate Fellowship of Christian Athletes chapter.

References available upon request.

Resume Checklist

Personal data
    name
    address
    telephone number
Career goal or job interest (optional)
Education
Employment history
Publications (optional)
Research (optional)
Activities and interests (optional)
Special skills (optional)
References

BUSINESS REPORTS

Business reports have two basic purposes:
1. To collect and interpret data so that an executive can make an informed decision
2. To communicate information to staff, stockholders, customers, or other concerned parties

The business report represents the best efforts of a company, and its appearance should reflect that fact.

Formal and Informal Reports

Formal reports are usually sent to customers or stockholders. They include printed covers and extensive charts. They are usually bound and attractively formatted. Informal reports are usually circulated to staff within a company. The pages may be stapled or paper-clipped together in the upper-left-hand corner. Before preparing a report, check with an executive to determine your company's house style.

Parts of the Business Report

Cover

The cover should be attractive as well as protective. A formal report cover may be a printed glossy illustration with the title printed on it. A cover for an informal report may consist of a typed page with the title printed in capital letters. A subtitle may be added after the title in one of two ways: (1) put a colon after the title and type the subtitle in capitals; (2) type the subtitle in lower case under the title:

THE 1995 CELLULAR PHONE MARKET:
SALES PROSPECTS FOR GEMCO

THE 1995 CELLULAR PHONE MARKET
Sales Prospects for Gemco

Flyleaf (formal report only)

Insert a blank page after the cover.

Title Fly (formal report only)

Type the report title in capitals in the upper third of the page as it appears on the cover.

Title Page

The title page may serve as the cover of a report—especially if it is an informal report. The title page consists of several blocks: (1) the title in capitals on the upper third of the page; (2) the writer's name, title, department or address; (3) the reader's name, title, and address; and (4) the date of completion. Usually these elements are centered on the page, with appropriate spaces between the blocks. Many styles are acceptable as long as the title page looks balanced and attractive. For informal or staff reports, the information may be briefer. (See page 181 for a sample.)

Letter of Authorization

A business report is often written in response to an order or a request for information from a person or a company. Include a copy of the letter that authorizes the report. (See page 183 for a sample.)

Letter of Transmittal

This letter serves as a foreword to the report. It should state the purpose of the report, the research methods, the limitations of the project, and the possibilities for the future. The letter should end with a note of thanks and willingness to be of further help. The tone should be positive and friendly. The letter of transmittal is typed on the letterhead stationery of the author of the report, who also signs it. (See page 184 for a sample.)

Acknowledgments (optional)

If others contributed to the preparation of the report, the author may wish to add a page acknowledging their help. The writer may add his or her initials or name.

The author wishes to thank the employees of McComber Graphics for their cooperation in preparing this report.

Jack Soguchi

Special thanks to Ms. Jeanette Lupi, who offered valuable assistance as a researcher, and to Ms. Harriet Podsnap, who edited the manuscript.

J. S.

Table of Contents

The table of contents guides the reader to specific topics in the report. It also serves as a brief outline of the report—its subjects and organization. The table of contents lists major topics and subtopics and page numbers. The contents page is often done last since it should indicate a complete listing of all material in the report. A table of contents should look well organized.

Type TABLE OF CONTENTS or CONTENTS in capitals, centered, at the top of the page:

TABLE OF CONTENTS

CONTENTS

Topic headings should appear in capitals on the left margin. Subtopics should be indented at least three spaces. Double-space before and after headings, but single-space between subtopic headings. If the report uses Roman numerals before topic headings and capital letters before subtopic headings, as in an outline, the Table of Contents should do the same.

To separate the topic and subtopic headings from the page numbers, use periods, dashes, or blank spaces. The first page of the section should be listed on the right margin. Several styles are acceptable:

List of Illustrations (optional)

If the report contains more than three charts, graphs, pictures, maps, or tables of statistics, compile a List of Illustrations. (If only one or two illustrations are included, the list may be included in the Table of Contents.) The form of the List of Illustrations should be the same as the Table of Contents. Type LIST OF ILLUSTRATIONS or ILLUSTRATIONS in capitals at the top center of the page.

ILLUSTRATIONS

LIST OF ILLUSTRATIONS

Assign a letter or number to each illustration as a guide to the reader. The letter or number should appear on the left-hand margin. The title of the illustration should be typed in capitals. The page number should be typed on the right-hand margin. Several styles are acceptable:

Table	Title	Page
I.	PHOTO OF PLANT SITE	17
II.	CONSTRUCTION COSTS	42
III.	STATISTICAL ABSTRACT	53

Table		
A.	PHOTO OF PLANT SITE	17
B.	CONSTRUCTION COSTS	42
C.	STATISTICAL ABSTRACT	53

Abstract (optional)

An abstract—also called a summary, synopsis, digest, or précis—is a brief review of the whole report. A busy executive may want to read quickly the major points and recommendations of the report without studying it in depth. If the letter of transmittal summarizes the major findings of the report, the abstract may be omitted. The abstract should not be longer than one page. (See page 185.)

Text

The text consists of an introduction, body, and conclusion. The report may be typed in paragraph form without breaks, or it may be divided into topics and subtopics with headings at the beginning of each section.

Headings

Headings make a business report easier to read by high-
lighting the organization. The headings should be coordi-
nated with the listings in the table of contents.

Some styles place the headings flush on the left margin. Others center major and minor topic headings. Two
blank lines separate the title and major and minor topic
headings. Paragraph headings are usually underlined and
indented five spaces and run into the text of the paragraph. Major topics are usually typed in capitals while
minor topics printed in lower case and underlined.
Outline form, based on the table of contents, may be
maintained:

I. MAJOR TOPIC

  A. Minor Topic
    1. Subtopic
      a. <u>Paragraph Heading</u>

Or, if the outline form is not used, the headings may
simply be typed without numbers or letters. Several styles
are acceptable:

MAJOR TOPIC
<u>Minor Topic</u>
Subtopic
    <u>Paragraph Heading</u>

MAJOR TOPIC
<u>Minor Topic</u>

Subtopic
    <u>Paragraph Heading</u>

Introduction

The introduction usually contains a brief history of the company and provides background for the report. It also includes a statement of purpose, which may include information on who authorized the report and why it was requested. In the introduction the writer seeks to justify the need for the report, documenting the problem, and suggesting the means by which it can be corrected. The writer of the report will also describe research methods, where and how information was obtained, and the limits of the assignment.

Body

The body of the report contains a discussion of the problem. It should be objective and balanced. Do not confine the discussion exclusively to support your position, but give consideration to other alternatives, including those that you do not recommend. Charts or tables of statistics may appear within the report to support your conclusion.

The discussion will vary with the specific subject. Try to organize the discussion by breaking it down into topics and subtopics. Most topics can be classified by alternatives, criteria, or similar categories. For example, a study of sites for a new business may be broken down into subtopics by criteria—retail market, population, construction costs—or by alternatives—Chicago, New York, or Los Angeles.

Conclusion

Conclusions or recommendations are usually found at the end of the report to give a sense that they are the final result of a well-built case. Conclusions or recommendations may also be stated at the very beginning of the report.

This section should state succinctly the most convincing reasons for recommending the choice of action. If several alternatives have been considered, do not neglect to point out their advantages or disadvantages. For emphasis state the recommendation in either the opening or closing sentence of this section.

Tables

Statistics and data in the text of a report can be confusing. For this reason data may be presented in the form of tables, charts, or graphs. This information can be presented within the text or in an Appendix at the end. If the data is presented in the text, it should be highlighted by a box, blank space, or a separate page.

Population of Potential Market Sites, 1990	
Cape Aaron	123,776
Johnstown	127,998
Lilahville	145,889

If the tables are included in the Appendix, you may refer the reader to the specific exhibit with a note in the text.

After five years, the cost savings of renting over building will be under $200, as Appendix C illustrates.

After five years, the cost savings of renting over building will be under $200. (See Appendix C.)

Footnotes

Footnotes indicate sources of information that are used in a report. Footnotes are used when words are quoted directly or ideas are borrowed in paraphrase. Less often, a footnote reports secondary information that the writer does not wish to include in the text. Do not clutter your text with footnotes.

A footnote is indicated by a number that appears at the end of the borrowed material. It is typed without a space, one third above the line. The footnote number should appear outside quotation marks:

George Fox in his annual economic forecast predicts "modest levels of growth with minimal inflationary pressures."[1]

Market trends, according to a report in <u>Sales Today</u>, will continue downward for the next three to five years.[2]

Footnotes are usually numbered consecutively (1,2,3,4....) throughout a report. Other styles start over again with the beginning of each page or chapter. The footnote itself may be typed on the bottom of the page, separated from the text by a line twenty spaces long that is typed from the left margin. More often, footnotes appear on a separate page at the end of the text marked NOTES or FOOTNOTES. For footnote style and placement, check the style sheet or manual preferred by your company.

Footnotes follow a basic form:

Books
> # Author's Name, Book Title (Place of
> Publication: Publisher, Date), p. #.

Magazines
> # Author's Name, "Title of Article," *Magazine*,
> #(Date), pp. #.

The footnote itself is usually indented six to seven spaces from the left margin. (Some styles start the footnote flush on the left margin.) First, type the footnote number. It may be raised one third above the line or typed directly on the line. If the number is typed on the line, a period after the number is optional. Next, leave a space. The second line is typed flush with the number. Several forms are acceptable, but be consistent. Use one form only throughout your report.

book author	1 Luis Sandoval, *The International Coal Trade* (New York: Moby Press, 19920, p. 18.
multiple authors	2 Frank Li and Yvette Lim, *Marketing Today* (Boston: Tharp Press, 1989), p. 213.
no author stated	3 "Grain Futures" *Food Industry Review*, XXI:17(April, 1990), 312.
article from magazine	4 Thomas Kucinski, "The Federal Reserve Board and Money Supply" *Financial News*, 18(May 27, 1990), 15.
unpublished	5 Terry Soter, personal letter of December 27, 1994.
	6 Anthony Valente, telephone interview, February 2, 1994.

Subsequent references to the same source do not have to copy the complete footnote. Instead, the author and page number will suffice:

7 Kucinski, p. 18.

If more than one book by the same author is footnoted, then add the title in the subsequent references:

8 Sandoval, *The International Coal Trade*, p. 221.

The Latin phrase "Ibid" (meaning "in the same place") may be used if a source is repeated consecutively in the footnotes:

9 Indra Patel, *Real Estate Investment in Developing Countries* (New York: Astor Press, 1989), p. 182.

10 Ibid., p. 193.

Appendix

An appendix contains background information that is not included in the body of the report. This includes graphs, charts, illustrations, documents, and so on. A separate sheet with the title *Appendix* typed in the center separates this section from the text of the report. You may also group the material into categories by typing a letter or number at the top of each page: Appendix A, Appendix B, Appendix C; or Appendix 1, Appendix 2, Appendix 3.

Bibliography

A bibliography is a list of all sources of information used to compile the report, whether or not the sources appear in the footnotes. The bibliography appears on a separate sheet at the end of the report. The bibliography is compiled alphabetically beginning with the author's last name or, if no author is stated, with the title.

A bibliographic listing contains essentially the same information as the footnote but in somewhat different form. The last name of the author appears first. Periods rather than commas are used to separate elements. All the pages of an article are listed, not just the specific page reference. (If the volume number is stated, it is not necessary to type "pp." before the page numbers.) Bibliographies follow a basic form:

> *book*   Last name, First name. *Title.* City of publication: Publisher, Date.
>
> *article*   Last name, First name. "Title." *Magazine,* vol.#(Date), pp.#-#.

To prepare a bibliography, type on the top of the page in capitals:

BIBLIOGRAPHY

Each reference is typed flush on the left margin. The second line is indented five to seven spaces. If the bibliography lists more than one work by a single author, subsequent references begin with a six-space line followed by a period rather than the author's name.

Sharp, Rebecca. *Successful Salesmanship.* New York: Vanity Press, 1978.

_____. *Sales and Marketing Today.* New York: Vanity Press, 1993.

Here are some sample bibliographic entries:

book	Podsnap, Marilyn. *The International Textile Trade.* Boston:Berkeley Press, 1992.
multiple authors	Smallweed, Harold and Turlington, Esther. *New Approaches to Retail Sales.* Atlanta: Peachtree Publications, 1991.
no author	"Microprocessors of Tomorrow." *Computer Reports.* 11 (May, stated 1994), 281-283.
article from a magazine	Kucinski, Bill. "The Federal Reserve Board and Money Supply." *Financial News.* 18 (August, 1993), 379-391.
unpublished material	Sirahata, Teri. Personal Letter, May 27, 1990. Valvano, Michael. Telephone Interview, June 6, 1993.

Typing Instructions for Reports

Margins

Left and right	1-1¼ inches (unbound)
	1½ inches (bound)
Top	2 inches on first page
	1 inch on all other pages
Bottom	1-1½ inches

Paragraphs

Paragraphs should be indented at least three spaces. Do not begin a paragraph on the last line of a page or hyphenate the last word in a paragraph. If a paragraph is typed on more than one page, make sure that the second page contains more than two lines of the paragraph.

Spacing

For ease of reading, business reports are usually double-spaced. Single-spacing is permissible but less preferable.

Quotes

Quoted or extracted material over three lines in length
may be single-spaced and indented at least five spaces on
the left and right margins. For example:

The sales director made several suggestions to the executive committee to improve performance. He stated,

> Aggressive marketing can demonstrably raise
> sales. We tend to be a bit lax, believing that our
> reputation will sell the product. I'd like to see us
> advertise the quality edge of our merchandise.

He continued to outline the components of an advertising campaign that he would recommend for the company.

Model Page for a Business Report

<u>TITLE</u>

(2 spaces)

MAJOR TOPIC

_____
_____
_____.

(2 spaces)

MINOR TOPIC

(2 SPACES)

_____
_____
_____.

(2 SPACES)

Subtopic

(1 space)

_____
_____
_____.

(2 spaces)

<u>Paragraph</u> <u>Heading</u>._____
_____
_____.

Sample Report

SITE SELECTION FOR A NEW RIVERVIEW HEALTH CLUB

Prepared by
Maceo Davis
Archway Consultants

for
Anthony Pesci, President
Riverview Health Clubs

December 27, 1994

TABLE OF CONTENTS

RIVERVIEW HEALTH CLUBS 12 Apache Drive Tuscon, Arizona 00000

March 17, 1994

Mr. Maceo Davis, Executive Director
Archway Consultants
78 Ridge Boulevard
Phoenix, AZ 00000

Dear Mr. Davis:

As I mentioned in our meeting of February 25, Riverview Health Clubs is
interested in expanding. We would like you to survey three locations in Seneca,
Walhalla, and Tougaloo and report to us on which site offers the best potential
market.

Riverview currently operates three facilities in Arizona. Our clubs are designed
for fitness and relaxation, and we offer facilities for our customers to work out on
exercise machines, engage in weight training, and relax in our fitness centers.
These centers contain saunas, whirlpools, and steam rooms.

We operate exercise clubs with the finest equipment and service. Our annual dues
are $750, so we will need to expand into an area that is relatively affluent.

As noted in our conversation, we would appreciate your report by May 15 so that
we can review it prior to our board meeting. Please call me if you need more
information or if you wish access to our records or facilities.

Yours truly,

Anthony Pesci, President

AP/dg

ARCHWAY CONSULTANTS
78 Ridge Boulevard
Phoenix, AZ 00000

May 4, 1994

Mr. Anthony Pesci, President
Riverview Health Clubs
12 Apache Drive
Tuscon, Arizona 00000

Dear Mr. Pesci:

As you requested in your letter of March 17, I have reviewed the market for a new River Health Club facility and have examined three sites in Seneca, Walhalla, and Tougaloo. Archway Consultants believes that your health and fitness center should be built at the shopping mall currently under construction in Tougaloo.

We reviewed the relative merits of each location relative to population, market characteristics, and facility costs. Seneca is the largest city, and Walhalla offers a stable business environment, but Tougaloo offers the best market for growth. As the mall in Tougaloo is now under construction, Riverview will be able to design a custom facility without large development and construction outlays.

I will be glad to meet with you to explain further our reasons for recommending the Tougaloo site. Please feel free to call me at your convenience.

Cordially,

Maceo Davis
Executive Director

SUMMARY

This report examined locations in Seneca, Walhalla, and Tougaloo to determine the best location for a new branch of the Riverview Health Club. After examining population characteristics, income levels, and the retail markets, Archway Consultants concluded that Tougaloo, a rapidly growing university and research center, offered the best opportunity for a profitable operation.

INTRODUCTION

Riverview Health Club operates multipurpose fitness and recreational centers that appeal to an increasingly health-conscious population. Since opening its first club in Tucson in 1984, Riverview has expanded to locations in Phoenix (1987) and Flagstaff (1991). All three units have proven profitable with net sales of over six million dollars in the 1994 fiscal year. Membership has grown rapidly, and the centers now operate at nearly full capacity, averaging almost six hundred members per location. Additional moneys are derived from guest fees, special user charges, rentals, and retail equipment sales. With annual membership dues of $750, Riverview Health Clubs appeal to an affluent population.

Statement of Purpose

Mr. Anthony Pesci, President of Riverview Health Clubs, has authorized Archway Consultants to conduct a site survey to determine the best location for Riverview's expansion. The three alternatives are 1) a converted warehouse in Seneca, 2) a construction site in Walhalla, and 3) a shopping mall in Tougaloo.

<u>Method</u>

Archway Consultants investigated each location by three criteria:

1. population
2. retail market
3. facilities.

Each location was studied to determine income levels of the population and potential growth trends. Archway also interviewed local developers, retailers, and Chamber of Commerce officials to gain a sense of the business climate in each area.

<u>Scope</u>

This report confines its investigation to parameters defined by Riverview Health Clubs. Alternative construction sites are available at each location, but are not reviewed here. The criteria established were deemed to be the most applicable, but other factors such as the relative age of the population may also influence the choice of a location.[1]

POPULATION

<u>Seneca</u>

The largest of the three cities, Seneca has a population of 143,672. Since the 1970s its population has been stable. The median income is a relatively high $29,567, but only a small percentage of its population (2.5) falls in the upper income bracket.

<u>Walhalla</u>

The population has experienced steady growth, but the metropolitan population of 133,876 is significantly smaller than Seneca's. Of all three sites Walhalla has the highest median income ($30,103), and a significant percentage of its population is affluent; 4.5 percent earn over $40,000 annually.

<u>Tougaloo</u>

Though it currently has the smallest population, Tougaloo has experienced rapid growth in the past twenty years. The population has nearly doubled since 1980 and now numbers 131,875. The median income of $29,350 is competitive with both Seneca and Walhalla. Almost 11 percent of its population is listed in the highest income bracket, reflecting the significant number of professionals who have moved to the area recently for the research park and state university complex.

Median Family Income, 1990	
Seneca	$29,567
Walhalla	30,103
Tougaloo	29,360
Source: Statistical Abstract of the Southwest	

RETAIL MARKET

<u>Seneca</u>

Retail sales have been in a prolonged slump, reflecting national economic trends. Ms. Felice Gonzalez, director of the Chamber of Commerce, described local business conditions as "generally flat."[2] The principal employer, Dedmon

4

Industries, has been phasing out its operation and transferring its administrative personnel. Data indicate that a large percentage of disposable income is spent on the home, food, and transportation rather than on recreation or entertainment.

Walhalla

The economic situation is stable. Retail sales have remained level for several years even as the national economy remains depressed. A significant proportion of the population at the upper income levels traditionally spends significantly on entertainment and recreation. Walhalla is a banking and financial center, and these institutions have proven to be secure, experiencing steady if limited growth. The white-collar population of Walhalla is significant.

Tougaloo

Once an agricultural market town, Tougaloo has the makings of a "booming post-industrial center."[3]   A state university campus established in 1965 has expanded rapidly to 18,500 students. A state-subsidized research park was opened in 1971 which has succeeded in attracting a mix of electronic and pharmaceutical firms including Fuchs Electronics, Ariel Computers, and Shirata Chemicals. The university and research park are drawing to the area a large and well-paid professional population. Median income, though slightly below Seneca and Walhalla, is rising dramatically, and this trend should continue. Data suggest that the Tougaloo population spends a large percentage of its disposable income on recreation and entertainment.

FACILITIES

Seneca

A refurbished warehouse is available downtown on South Street. The building offers 15,000 square feet of floor space, sufficient for offices, fitness center, and exercise and locker rooms. Rental should be approximately $8 per square foot, or $120,000 annually. A two-year lease is available. The building would require major renovation. Another problem is the lack of parking space as only a nearby municipal lot, which charges $.50 per hour, could handle the expected flow of traffic. The downtown location would appeal strongly to office workers and commuters but would be less attractive to suburbanites.

Walhalla

The site is currently an open lot located on Route 17, a major thoroughfare. The building could be designed to Riverview's specifications, but current construction costs of $50 per square foot would require a large cash outlay. Conveniently located near an exit to the I-90 beltway, the site offers easy access to major subdivisions and retail and office complexes. It is situated on the town's north side which is the area of greatest suburban growth.

Tougaloo

The site is in a major shopping mall now under construction. The building currently has 41,000 square feet of unrented space, and Mr. Sam Woodfin, sales agent for Bestworth Developers, has stated that he would work with Riverview in designing facilities. Rentals should be $9 per square foot. The mall has already received commitment from a major luxury department story--Heyman's--as well as several dry-good franchises that cater to an affluent clientele. The mall is located at the intersection of Interstate 15 and Route 301. A development of 300 "luxury town houses" is now under construction three miles from the mall.

6

RECOMMENDATIONS

Archway Consultants recommends that Riverview Health Clubs open the new branch in Tougaloo. It best meets the requirements of population, facilities, and retail market.

Seneca

The city offers a large population base, but its economy is stagnant. Few data indicate that the trends will improve. The site is inconvenient to Riverview's consumer market, and the facility has shortcomings, especially with parking.

Walhalla

This site is an attractive choice with a stable population and sound economic base. The area is currently the most affluent of the three alternatives. Developing the Walhalla site, however, will require substantial development costs.

Tougaloo

Though the smallest in population, Tougaloo offers the greatest opportunity for growth. The trend indicates rapid expansion of the local economy with an affluent, active population. The mall site can be tailored to fit Riverview's needs at minimal cost. For these reasons Archway Consultants strongly recommends that the new Riverview Health Club be located in the Tougaloo mall.

NOTES

1 Archway Consultants recommends that Riverview Health Clubs consider a survey of its members to draw a more detailed statistical profile of its potential consumer market.

2 Felice Gonzalez, interview held at the Seneca Chamber of Commerce, March 23, 1993.

3 Thomas Hechinger, *Tougaloo: A City for Tomorrow* (Phoenix: Arrowhead Press, 1992), p. 17.

APPENDIX
Population

	1970	1980	1990
Seneca	141,506	142,891	143,672
Walhalla	121,613	128,403	133,876
Tougaloo	91,312	113,645	131,598

Family Income by Percentage, 1990

	under 20,000	20,000-25,000	25,000-30,000	30,000-40,000	over 40,000
Seneca	29.6	15.9	14.0	28.0	12.5
Walhalla	20.6	15.6	15.1	33.6	15.5
Tougaloo	15.4	15.1	15.2	37.5	17.1

Distribution of Disposable Income by Percentage, 1990

	Food	Housing	Transport	Clothing	Medical	Recreation
Seneca	30.8	18.6	9.0	9.2	4.2	10.5
Walhalla	24.1	22.1	9.1	7.6	5.6	11.6
Tougaloo	20.4	22.5	8.0	7.4	3.9	14.7

Source: U.S. Census Bureau Statistics

BIBLIOGRAPHY

Banks, John. Editor. *Economic Survey of the Sunbelt*. Houston: Longhorn
      Publications, 1992.

Gonzalez, Felice. Interview. Seneca Chamber of Commerce, March 23, 1993.

Hechinger, Thomas. *Tougaloo: A Community for Tomorrow*. Phoenix:
      Arrowhead Press, 1992.

Hung, Lee. "Marketing Opportunities in Recreation." *Southwest Business
      Review*. 28(April, 1993), 17-29.

Seneca Chamber of Commerce. *Economic Prospects for the Nineties*. Seneca:
      Woodside Printers, 1992.

United States Bureau of the Census. *Statistical Abstract of the United States,
      1991*. Washington: United States Government Printing Office, 1991.

Business Report Checklist

Cover (optional)
Flyleaf (optional)
Title fly (optional)
Title page
Letter of authorization
Letter of transmittal
Acknowledgments (optional)
Table of contents
List of tables or illustrations (optional)
Abstract (Summary or Précis)
Text
Footnotes (optional)
Appendix (optional)
Bibliography (optional)

BASIC PUNCTUATION

Period (.)

1. A period marks the end of a statement that is a complete sentence:

    The American automobile industry reported record sales.

    After the chairman resigned, the board expanded its membership.

2. A period marks the end of an indirect question:

    The director wondered if the staff would accept the new policy.

3. A period follows an abbreviation:

Mr.	Mrs.	Ms.
Jan.	Feb.	Mon.
etc.	tbs.	yd.
Co.	Inc.	Ltd.

4. If an abbreviation represents more than one word, a period follows each initial:

M.D.	U.S.A.	Ph.D.

196

5. Official Postal Service codes do not include periods:

NY   CA   SD

Some organizations do not use periods when their titles are abbreviated:

FCC   FDA   AARP

6. When an abbreviation ends a sentence, use one period:

He moved to Boston from Charleston, S.C.

Question Mark (?)

Use a question mark at the end of a direct question:

When can we meet to discuss this issue?
Where are the travel vouchers?

Exclamation Point (!)

To emphasize a dramatic statement or a strongly held view, end with an exclamation point:

Act now!
We beat the deadline!
Buy now or pay more later!

Quotation marks (" ") (' ')

1. Quotation marks precede and follow direct quotations.

Staff director Francis Wong asked, "Can exceptions be made to company policy on sick leave?"

> "Extremely low" interest rates should continue to bring "record high" earnings for the bank, according to the report.

2. Quotation marks are usually placed outside other punctuation marks with the exception of semicolons.

> The new advertising campaign has been called "negative," but I prefer to call it "aggressive."

> He said that the firm will replace "all defective parts"; labor costs are not included.

3. Quotation marks are not used at the end of an indirect quotation.

> They asked when delivery could be expected.

4. Quotation marks set off titles of short works:

> "Management Today" is the best feature in *Business Trade* magazine.

5. Single quotation marks indicate a quote within a quote:

> Frank Balducci said of the merger talks that he "opposed the process at the start but 'all's well that ends well.'"

Capitalization

1. Civic organizations and governmental bodies frequently are capitalized:

> CETA   UCLA   NAACP   NCAA   FBI

2. Complete quotations begin with a capital letter:

> Harold Levine stated, "All purchase orders must be authorized."

3. The first part of a split quotation begins with a capital letter, but the second part starts with a lower-case letter:

"I supported a higher dividend at first," the comptroller stated, "but now I cannot justify it."

Semicolon (;)

1. A semicolon may be used to join two independent clauses in place of a conjunction (or, and, but):

Sales figures rose; profit margins declined.
The staff was exhausted; the meeting was adjourned.

2. Long items in a series can be separated by semicolons:

First the supervisor resigned, and the manager applied for her position; then the assistant manager requested a transfer; finally, the sales staff requested a meeting with senior management.

3. Items in a series with internal commas are separated with semicolons for clarity:

The parcels were shipped to Rutherford, New Jersey; Dix Hills, New York; and Del Mar, California.

Colon (:)

1. A colon is used at the end of a complete sentence to indicate a list follows:

We need to order new office supplies: forms, stationery, and envelopes.

A fundraising campaign would accomplish the following objectives: raise faculty salaries, provide student scholarships, and improve facilities.

2. A colon is not used when the list follows an incomplete statement. Do *not* use a colon in the following situations:

We need to order stationery, envelopes, and business forms.

A fundraising campaign would raise faculty salaries, provide student scholarships, and improve facilities.

Comma (,)

1. Commas separate three or more items in a series:

We need to raise productivity, improve quality, and expand marketing.

2. Commas separate independent clauses joined by conjunctions.

Imperial Oil stock has risen sharply, but Pepco has remained flat.

Gloria Peebles is taking maternity leave, and Stanley Farshimi will handle her accounts until she returns.

3. When a sentence begins with a dependent clause, place a comma at the end:

After I consult the architect, I will call a board meeting.

4. Place commas around *yes* and *no*.

> Yes, the company will transfer its headquarters.
> As for layoffs, no, we will not decrease staff.

5. Words that interrupt the flow of a sentence are set off by commas:

> I agree, however, that budgetary pressures will continue.
> As you will agree, I think, our sales prospects are not all bleak.
> The southwest, for instance, is a region that is expected to grow.

6. Use commas to set off clauses or phrases that are not essential to the meaning of the sentence:

> The foreman, complaining of assembly-line delays, has requested a meeting with management.
> Infonet, which is headquartered in Rapid City, has made a bid to acquire Cableworks.

7. Commas separate each item in an address or date:

> Route 3, Box 439, Hillsborough, North Carolina

9. A comma follows an introductory word or phrase:

> Basically, I am satisfied with my job.
> In any case, the prosecutor has ordered an end to the investigation.

Dash (—)

1. Long comments that interrupt the flow of the sentence may be set off by dashes, especially if the comment is a sentence itself:

> No matter how far sales decline—and I know the figures are depressing—I think that we should proceed as planned.

2. Use dashes before and after a phrase or clause that has been set off by commas and has internal punctuation of its own:

> The most popular specials—tuna melt, beef stew, and clam chowder—should be on the menu daily.
>
> All our warranties—which, I should remind you, are legal obligations—must be honored at all costs.

3. A dash can emphasize an afterthought, clarification, or qualification:

> The company should expand now—or pay later.
> We have only one option—sell.

4. A list of terms may be set off by a dash rather than a colon:

> Each faculty member has specific responsibilities—teaching, research, and administration.

Note: The dashes in the examples above are typeset dashes called "em" dashes; a typewriter or word processor equivalent may be formed by typing two hyphens with no space between the word and hyphen.

Apostrophe (')

1. Apostrophes indicate possession:

   Loretta's computer   today's temperature

2. Plural words ending -s and singular words of more than one syllable ending -es use only an apostrophe to show possession:

   the Arabs' history   officers' quarters
   Los Angeles' pollution   Frances' desk

3. Apostrophes indicate contractions:

   don't (do not)   can't (cannot)
   I'm (I am)   aren't (are not)

Ellipsis (...)

1. Use ellipsis—three periods—to show that words are omitted from a quotation:

   The consultant reported that "company prospects look bright . . . if you take steps to cut costs now."

2. When ellipsis concludes a sentence, add a fourth period:

   He started to name the states which have enacted anti-smog legislation: Virginia, New York, California, Florida, Maine. . . .

GRAMMAR TROUBLESHOOTING

1. A singular subject takes a singular verb no matter what phrases intervene:

> The department with the most employees needs
> to reduce staff.
> The certificate, including the endorsements,
> looks counterfeit.
> The chairman, as well as the board members,
> wants to revise the policy.

2. A collective noun may be either singular or plural, depending on whether it is taken as a unit or as parts.

> The team agrees with the coach.
> The team disagree among themselves.
>
> The jury files out as a group.
> The jury file out one by one.

3. Some words are singular in meaning while plural in form and take singular verbs:

> Physics is a requirement for graduation.
> The news is good.
> The United Nations helps keep world peace.

4. Subject words with *-one* or *-body* (*one, anyone, someone, anybody, everybody, somebody, nobody, none, no one*) are singular:

> One is enough.
> Everyone is invited.
> Nobody has the answer.

5. The words *either* and *neither* are singular when used as subjects of a sentence:

> Either is satisfactory.
> Neither has permission to leave.

6. In sentences with *either . . . or* and *neither . . . nor* the verb agrees with the subject that is closer:

> Either two rooms or a suite is adequate.
> Neither a credit nor a refund was offered.

7. *Each* is singular; *both* is plural.

> Each of the managers has requested a transfer.
> Both have requested transfers.

8. Number and person in a sentence must remain consistent:

> The *doctors* must file *their* insurance forms immediately.
> The *doctor* must file *his* or *her* insurance form immediately.
> *Everyone* must report daily to *his* or *her* supervisor.

Note: To avoid wordy or awkward phrasing, some style sheets allow a plural pronoun to be used with *everyone* or *everybody*, especially in informal writing:

> *Everyone* must report daily to *their* supervisors.

9. Tense (past, present, future) must be consistent:

> We were late, and we rescheduled the meeting.
> We are running late, and we are rescheduling the meeting.
> We will be late, and we will reschedule the meeting.

10. Avoid dangling words or phrases:

> *wrong:* Hopefully, we'll finish the project.
> *corrected:* I am hopeful that we'll finish the project.

> *wrong:* Merging with its competitor, the price of Comet stock rose.
> *corrected:* Merging with its competitor, Comet saw the price of its stock rise.

11. Place a modifier as close as possible to the word it modifies:

> *wrong:* The car hit the stop sign speeding out of control.
> *corrected:* Speeding out of control, the car hit the stop sign.

> *wrong:* He gave his resignation to the manager in writing.
> *corrected:* He gave his resignation in writing to the manager.

12. Use adjectives to modify nouns and pronouns, and adverbs to modify verbs, adjectives, and other adverbs:

> *wrong:* He did the job good.
> *corrected:* He did the job well.

13. Note irregular adjectives:

positive	*comparative*	*superlative*
good	better	best
bad	worse	worst
much	more	most
little	less	least

14. Note irregular adverbs:

positive	*comparative*	*superlative*
well	better	best
badly	worse	worst
much	more	most
little	less	least

FORMS OF ADDRESS

Person	Envelope	Salutation
Ambassador, American	The Honorable Name, American Ambassador Address City, State	Sir: Madam: Dear Mr. Ambassador: Dear Madam Ambassador:
Ambassador, foreign	His (Her) Excellency Name, Ambassador of Country Address Washington, DC	Excellency: Dear Mr. Ambassador: Dear Madam Ambassador: My dear Mr. Name: My dear Madam Name:
Archbishop, Roman Catholic	The Most Reverend Name Archbishop of City Address City, State	Most Reverend and dear Sir: Dear Archbishop Name: Your Excellency: Reverend Sir:

Person	Envelope	Salutation
Bishop, Episcopal	The Right Reverend Name Bishop of Diocese Address City, State	Right Reverend Sir: Dear Bishop Name:
Bishop, Methodist	Bishop Name Address City, State	My dear Bishop Name: Dear Bishop Name:
Bishop, Roman Catholic	The Most Reverend Name Bishop of Diocese Address City, State	Your Excellency: Most Reverend Sir: Dear Bishop Name:
Cabinet Officer, United States	The Honorable Name The Secretary of [Dept.] Address City, State	Sir: Madam: Dear Mr. Secretary: Dear Madam Secretary: Dear Mr. Name: Dear Mrs. Name:

Person	Envelope	Salutation
Cardinal, Roman Catholic	His Eminence Given Name Cardinal: Surname Archbishop of City Address City, State	Your Eminence: My dear Cardinal: Dear Cardinal Surname:
Clergyman, Protestant[a] (except Episcopal)	The Reverend (Dr.) Name Address City, State	My dear Mr. (Dr.): Dear Mr. Name: Dear Pastor Name:
Consul	Full Name, Esq. Country Consul Street address City, State	Sir: Madam: Dear Mr(s). Consul:
Dean, College	Dean (or Dr.) Name College University City, State	Sir: Madam: Dear Dean Name: Dear Dr. Name

210

Person	Envelope	Salutation
Doctor	Dr. Name, or Full Name, M.D., Ph.D., or D.D. Street address City, State	Dear Dr. Name
Governor	The Honorable Name Governor of State Address City, State	Sir: Madam: My dear Governor Name: Dear Governor Name:
Imam	Imam Address City, State	Dear Imam Name: Dear Imam:
Judge	The Honorable Name Name of Court Address City, State	Sir: Madam: My dear Judge Name: Dear Judge Name:

Person	Envelope	Salutation
Legislator	The Honorable Name Name of Legislative Body Address City, State	Sir: Madam: Dear Senator Name: My dear Mr(s).: Dear Mr(s).: Dear Ms.:
Mayor	The Honorable Name Mayor of City Address City, State	Sir: Madam: Dear Mayor Name:
Military Officer	Rank Name Address City, State	Sir: Madam: Dear General (Admiral, Major, Captain) Name:
Monsignor, Roman Catholic	The Reverend Dr. Name: or The Right Reverend Monsignor Name Address City, State	Right Reverend and dear Monsignor Name: My Reverend and dear Monsignor Name: Dear Monsignor Name:

Person	Envelope	Salutation
Nun	Sister Religious Name, Initials of Order Address City, State	My dear Sister: Dear Sister Religious Name:
Patriarch, Eastern Orthodox	His Beatitude the Patriarch of Diocese Address City, State	Most Reverend Lord:
Pope	His Holiness the Pope Vatican City Rome, Italy	Your Holiness: Most Holy Father:
President, College or University	President Full Name, or Dr. Full Name College or University City, State	Sir: Madam: Dear Dr. Name: Dear President Name:

213

Person	Envelope	Salutation
President, United States	The President The White House Washington, DC	Mr. President: Dear Mr. President: Dear President Name:
President, Prime Minister (foreign country)	President Name, or Prime Minister Name Address City, Country	Excellency: Dear Mr. President: Dear Mr. President: Madam Prime Minister:
Priest, Roman Catholic, Episcopal	The Reverend (Dr.) Name Address	Reverend and dear Sir: My dear Father Name: Dear Father:
Professor	Prof. Name Department of Subject College or University City, State	Dear Sir: Dear Madam: Dear Professor Name: Dear Dr. Name:

214

Person	Envelope	Salutation
Rabbi	Rabbi Name Address City, State	Dear Rabbi Name: Dear Dr. Name:
Representative	The Honorable Name The House of Representatives Washington, DC	Sir: Madam: Dear Mr.: Dear Mrs: Dear Ms.:
Senator	The Honorable Name United States Senate Washington, DC	Sir: Madam: Dear Senator Name:
Sheik	Sheik Name Address City, State	Dear Sheik Name:

Person	Envelope	Salutation
Supreme Court Justice	The Honorable Name, Associate (or Chief) Justice of the United States Supreme Court Washington, DC	Sir: Madam: Mr(s). Justice: Dear Mr(s). Justice: Dear Mr(s). Justice Name:
United Nations Representative	His (or Her) Excellency, Country Representative to the United Nations United Nations New York, NY	Excellency: Your Excellency: Ambassador: Sir: Madam: Mr(s). Name:
Vice President	The Vice President Washington, DC	Sir: Madam: Dear Mr. Vice President: Dear Mr. Name:

MAILING

Businesses now have available a variety of mail services for both domestic and international mail. Alternative delivery services such as UPS or Federal Express offer overnight or two-day service for letters, documents, or small packages. These firms have collection boxes or can arrange pick-up. They also have limits as to the size and weight of the package that they will deliver. The United States Postal Service offers a wide variety of mailing options. Check to see if your firm keeps an account with a specific agency or has a set policy on mailings.

Classes

First Class

First class is commonly used for letters, post cards, checks, and money orders. If the first-class mail is not letter size, mark First Class on the envelope or use a large envelope with a green border. The Postal Service may not open first-class mail sent within the United States without a search warrant. First-class mail cannot be insured, but a certificate of mailing, certified, return receipt, or restricted delivery is available at additional cost.

First-class mail is shipped by the fastest transportation available. It will generally be delivered overnight to designated cities and in two days to designated states. Beyond 600 miles the delivery standard is three days.

Priority Mail

Priority mail is for first-class mail that weighs more than 11 ounces but less than 70 pounds. The package must not exceed 108 inches in total length and circumference. All envelopes or packages sent by this class should be marked with free Priority Mail stickers available at the post office. Insurance can be purchased for Priority Mail.

Second Class

Second-class mail is generally used by publishers and registered news agents for the bulk mailing of periodicals or newspapers. The general public must use single-piece, third- or fourth-class rates for mailing magazines or newspapers.

Third Class

Third class is also known as bulk business or advertising mail. It is most often used for mass mailing by businesses or community organizations. Individuals may also use third class for light-weight parcels. Third-class parcels and printed matter must weigh under 16 ounces. There are separate single-piece and bulk rates. Insurance can be purchased for this class. Third-class service is slower than first-class, priority mail, or express mail.

Fourth Class

Fourth-class mail, also known as parcel post, is used for packages weighing from one to 70 pounds and measuring up to 108 inches in combined length and circumference. If a letter or other first-class material is enclosed, separate postage must be paid. This service has special rates for books, catalogues, and international mailings. Fourth-class mail can also be insured. Coast-to-coast delivery may take up to eight days using available transportation.

Express Mail

Express Mail is the Postal Service's fastest service. For Express Mail Next Day Service the mail must be taken to the post office generally by 5:00 PM or deposited in an Express Mail collection box. The mail will be delivered by 3:00 PM the following day, including weekends and holidays, or it can be picked up by 10:00 AM on the next day that the post office is open. Merchandise is automatically insured up to $500 against loss or damage while currency or bullion is limited to $15. Document reconstruction insurance is available up to $50,000 for non-negotiable documents. Other Express Mail services include Same Day Airport Service, Express Mail Custom Designed Service, and Express Mail International Service.

Special Delivery

Special delivery is available for all mail classes except bulk third class. Special delivery mail will be delivered beyond the hours of regular mail delivery, including Sundays and holidays. This service is offered to customers located on routes serviced by city carriers and to others who live within a one-mile radius of the post office. This mail must be marked "Special Delivery."

Special Handling

Special-handling service is available for third- and fourth-class mail. The mail will be given preferential handling in dispatch and transportation, but will not be given special delivery. Special handling does not afford protection for breakable items, which should be marked "FRAGILE."

Proof of Mailing and Delivery

Certificate of Mailing

A certificate of mailing is a receipt issued by the post office to indicate that a parcel has been mailed. A certificate of mailing does not provide insurance nor does the post office maintain a record of the transaction.

Certified Mail

Certified mail provides the sender with a mailing receipt, and the receiving post office maintains a record of delivery. This service is available only for first-class mail.

Return Receipt

A return receipt, which indicates proof of delivery, is available for mail sent registered, certified, COD, Express, or insured for more than $50. The return receipt indicates the delivery date and the name of the signer. At extra cost the receipt will show the exact address of delivery or request restricted delivery.

Restricted Delivery

On all services except Express Mail, the sender can request restricted delivery when purchasing a return receipt. The delivery will then be made only to the addressee or to a person who has written authorization to be an agent of the addressee. The written authorization requirement is waived for the agent when the addressee is a government official, a member of the legislature or judiciary of federal or state governments, a minor, or a person under guardianship.

Insurance

Registered Mail may be insured to a maximum of $25,000. Third- and fourth-class mail or mail mailed at the Priority or First-Class Mail rates has a $500 limit. The recipient signs a receipt of delivery which is filed at the delivery post office for articles insured for over $50.

Registered Mail

Registered mail, intended for valuable or important parcels, is the Postal Service's most secure means of delivery. Registered merchandise is controlled from mailing to delivery. Registered mail requires first-class postage and insurance may be purchased to a maximum of $25,000. Return receipt and restricted delivery service are available.

Collect on Delivery (COD)

COD service is available for merchandise sent first-, third-, or fourth-class, or registered mail. The addressee must have ordered the item. The COD fee includes insurance protection. COD service is limited to merchandise valued at no more than $500.

Money Orders

Money orders offer a means to avoid sending cash through the mail. Domestic money orders are available up to $700. The post office will replace lost or stolen money orders upon presentation of the receipt. The post office keeps copies of paid money orders for two years after the date paid.

International Mail

Airmail and surface mail service is available to almost all foreign countries. International mail has four categories:

1. Letters and Cards, including letters, letter packages, aerogrammes, and post cards;
2. Other Articles, including printed material, matter for the blind, and small packages;
3. Parcel Post;
4. Express Mail International Service

Registry service with limited reimbursement is available for letters and cards to most countries. Insurance for parcel post is also available for most countries.

POSTAL SERVICE ABBREVIATIONS

States

Alabama	AL	Maryland	MD	Oklahoma	OK
Alaska	AK	Massachu-		Oregon	OR
Arizona	AZ	setts	MA	Pennsyl-	
Arkansas	AR	Michigan	MI	vania	PA
California	CA	Minnesota	MN	Rhode Island	RI
Colorado	CO	Mississippi	MS	South Caro-	
Connecticut	CT	Missouri	MO	lina	SC
Delaware	DE	Montana	MT	South Da-	
District of		Nebraska	NE	kota	SD
Columbia	DC	Nevada	NV	Tennessee	TN
Florida	FL	New Hamp		Texas	TX
Georgia	GA	shire	NH	Utah	UT
Hawaii	HI	New Jersey	NJ	Vermont	VT
Idaho	ID	New		Virginia	VA
Illinois	IL	Mexico	NM	Washing-	
Indiana	IN	New York	NY	ton	WA
Iowa	IA	North Caro-		West Vir-	
Kansas	KS	lina	NC	ginia	WV
Kentucky	KY	North Da-		Wisconsin	WI
Louisiana	LA	kota	ND	Wyoming	WY
Maine	ME	Ohio	OH		

United States Territories and Dependencies

Canal Zone	CZ	Puerto Rico	PR
Guam	GU	Virgin Islands	VI

Canadian Provinces

Alberta	AB	Nova Scotia	NS
British		Ontario	ON
Columbia	BC	Prince	
Labrador	LB	Edward	
Manitoba	MB	Island	PE
New Bruns-		Quebec	PQ
wick	NB	Saskatche-	
Newfound		wan	SK
land	NF	Yukon	
Northwest		Territory	YT
Territories	NT		

GLOSSARY OF BASIC BUSINESS TERMS

A

account, (1) a ledger that shows a record of debits and credits; (2) a person or company to whom credit is extended or with whom business is done

amortization, (1) reduction of debt by making gradual payments on interest and capital; (2) reduction of the value of assets by extending the depreciation over a fixed period

annuity, periodical income from life insurance, retirement system, or investment which the person receives after years of contribution to the plan

antitrust law, legislation designed to increase competition by eliminating monopolies that restrain trade

appraisal, an evaluation of the worth of goods, assets, or property

appraise, to evaluate the worth of goods, assets, or property for taxes, sale, insurance, etc.

arbitrage, the immediate purchase of a security on one market and resale of the security or its equivalent on another market, earning a quick profit from the price discrepancy

arbitration, a procedure for settling disputes in which an impartial third party, the arbitrator, makes a decision binding on the disputing parties

arrears, money, interest, or dividends that are not paid when due; an account, a person, or a company is said to be *in arrears*

assets, any property that is owned and has monetary value

B

balance, (1) calculation of the difference between credits and debits of an account; (2) payment of an amount due; (3) the amount of credit in an account; (4) to equalize numbers, materials, weights, etc.

balanced budget, a budget without a surplus or a deficit, where expenditures equal revenues

balance of payments, a record of statistics that indicates economic transactions between countries over a fixed period

balance of trade, the difference between the value of a country's imported merchandise and exported merchandise

balance sheet, a statement that lists assets and liabilities of an organization at a given time

barter, the exchange of goods or services without money

bear, (1) a trader who sells short, making a profit when the market declines; (2) a business pessimist

bear market, a market with falling prices

bill of lading, a document issued to a shipper by a carrier that acknowledges receipt of goods, itemizes them, and specifies terms, place, and time of delivery

bill of sale, a receipt signed by the owner that specifies the legal transfer of property to the buyer

bond, (1) a note certifying that a business or government will pay the holder a certain sum with stated interest on a particular date; (2) the legal obligation of one party to guarantee payment or performance by a second party; (3) the value of a corporation based on its total assets less its debts

book value, (1) the value of a company's assets as recorded on the financial books of the company, in contrast to intrinsic or market value; (2) the value of a corporation based on its total assets less its debts

bourse, the French term for a stock exchange, often used abroad

broker, an agent who buys or sells bonds, stocks, or commodities for others on commission

bull, (1) a trader who tries to profit by rising prices; (2) a business optimist

bulletin board, a subscription computer service that displays news, messages, and information and provides access to other subscribers

bull market, market with rising prices

buy back, a company's repurchase of controlling interest of its stock at open market prices

buyer, a representative of a retail company who selects and purchases merchandise for a store

buyer's market, a market situation with abundant supply where purchasers can dictate price or terms of sale

buy in, outsider's purchase of controlling interest of a company's stock

buy on margin, to buy securities using credit from the broker as partial payment

buyout, the purchase of controlling shares of a company by employees or an outside company

C

calendar year, the twelve months from January 1 to December 31

call, (1) an option to buy a specific number of shares at a stated price within a certain time limit; (2) to demand payment; (3) to give notice that securities will be redeemed on a specific date

capital, (1) the total assets of a company; (2) money invested by owners to finance production; (3) money available for investment

capital gain, profit earned through the sale of securities, real estate, etc.

capital loss, moneys lost through the sale of securities, real estate, etc.

carrier, a business organization that transports people or merchandise

carrying charge, an additional fee paid by a customer to cover the cost of interest, service, credit, etc.

cartel, an association of producers or dealers who agree to control prices, limit production, divide territory, etc.

certificate of deposit (CD), a bank document indicating that the holder has made a time deposit, the sum of which will be left in the bank for a specific period

charter, (1) a document from a legislature or government body that confers rights and obligations on a bank or corporation; (2) the articles of a corporation; (3) to lease or hire for temporary use

chattel, (1) personal property; any property other than real estate; (2) property that is movable

clearing house, an association of banks and brokers which settles claims among its members

close corporation, a corporation controlled by a few stockholders with little or no public sale of shares

closed shop, a business that hires only union workers

closing price, the amount of the last sale of a security on one market day

collateral, property, cash, or redeemable security that a creditor offers to guarantee repayment of a loan

commerce, buying, trading, or selling goods and services

commission, the fee charged by an agent or broker for a sale, usually based on a percentage of price

commodity, (1) any goods that are physical and capable of being transported; (2) a product of trade—usually an agricultural product or a raw material—that is negotiated on a commodity exchange

common carrier, an organization that transports people or merchandise at government-regulated fixed rates

common stock, a security that indicates a share of ownership in a corporation with a claim on dividends and assets after settlement of claims by holders of preferred stock

competition, a market where a seller engages in a rivalry for profits and share of sales with other sellers

compound interest, interest that is paid on both original principal and the accrued unpaid interest

consignment, a type of sale in which the owner of a property authorizes an agent to sell the property for a fee or commission

consolidation, the union of two or more organizations into a single firm

consumer price index, a monthly governmental survey of retail prices based on a national sample

contract, an agreement between two or more parties that carries a legal obligation to perform according to certain terms

convertible, (1) bonds that can be exchanged for stock by the owner or the issuing company; (2) currency that can be exchanged for silver or gold or for the currency of a foreign country

corporation, a group of stockholders who form an association that is regarded legally as a single person

cosigner, a person who agrees to sign a note with another party and thus assumes obligations if the other party defaults

cover, the purchase of a security as compensation when selling short

credit, the ability to receive money, goods, or services against the promise of later payment

credit rating, an evaluation of a person or company based on net worth and history of meeting obligations

cut back, to halt or reduce production

D

debenture (bond), a bond backed by a company's general credit or good faith, not by specific property

deed, a legal document that conveys ownership of real estate

demand deposit, a bank deposit that can be withdrawn at any time

depreciate, to spread proportionally the cost of an asset over the time of its use

depreciation, the decline in value of property over time through use and age

discount, (1) an advanced deduction from a price by a wholesaler or retailer to someone who pays cash, pays early, or buys in quantity; (2) the amount that the face value of a security exceeds its market value; (3) interest on a loan that is collected in advance by deducting it from the amount of the loan

discount rate, (1) the minimum rate of lending; (2) the rate that the Federal Reserve Bank charges to member banks for loans

dividend, (1) corporate profits distributed to shareholders according to the size of their holdings; (2) moneys paid by certain savings associations as a type of interest or by insurance companies as a refund for overpayment

draft, a written order, such as a check, by which the writer authorizes a second party to make payment to a third party at the writer's expense

E

electronic mail (e-mail), a file or message transmitted on a computer network from one person to another person

endorsement, indorsement, (1) a signature on a document; (2) the signature on the back of a title or check that guarantees the transfer of property; (3) alterations in the original terms of an insurance policy

entrepreneur, a person who takes the risk to start, manage, and own a business

equity, (1) the net worth of a firm, the amount that assets exceed liabilities; (2) the body of laws, supplementary to legal statutes, that apply to injustice and unfair practices

escape clause, a stipulation in a contract that permits a party to avoid certain undesirable consequences

escrow, a deed, contract, or other valuable document that is deposited with a third party pending performance of some specific action

exchange, (1) to trade services or products; (2) the place where traders buy and sell commodities or securities

exchange rate, the price at which the currency of one country can buy the currency of another

excise tax, a tax that a government levies on products (usually luxury goods) produced or distributed within its territory

expense, (1) a cost to a business to operate or produce a good or service; (2) the general operating costs over an accounting period

F

fax, a system that allows facsimiles of documents to be transmitted electronically over telephone lines from one user to another

fee, (1) payment for a service; (2) title of ownership of real estate

fiduciary, (1) a trustee of an estate or organization; (2) a transaction conducted on the basis of good faith without collateral

fiscal year, the twelve-month accounting period

fixed charges, expenses such as rent, interest, and taxes which must be paid periodically regardless of business income

float, (1) in banking, the value of checks between the writing and collecting; (2) stock that is held for speculation rather than investment and is frequently traded; (3) an unfunded debt or unsold part of an offering of securities

foreclosure, a legal proceeding that requires the sale or forfeiture of a mortgaged property when the mortgagor is unable to pay the debt

franchise, a right granted by a government to a person or firm to conduct a specific business at a stated place and time

free and clear, titles (usually of real estate) with no lien or mortgage

frozen assets, securities, properties, or moneys of a business that cannot be sold quickly without great loss

funded debt, debt in the form of a bond or other long-term note

fungible goods, products that come in standard units—such as grain or coffee—which can be negotiated one for the other

futures, contracts for securities or commodities that are bought and sold for later delivery

G

gold standard, use of gold to back the value of monetary units, such as the system prevailing in the United States before 1934

goodwill, the intangible assets of a business based on reputation, consumer relations, quality of service, etc.

greenmail, the legal practice of buying stock in a company in the threat of a hostile takeover, forcing the company's management to purchase stock (inflating its price) to retain control

gross income, total gains or receipts before deductions

gross profit, total receipts beyond the cost of goods sold without deducting for expenses

H

hardware, the components of a a computer including processor, monitor, terminals, drives, printer, and so on

hedging, buying and selling to reduce the risk of loss

holding company, a corporation that owns enough shares in other firms to control them

hostile takeover, a predatory bid or merger proposal that is contrary to the wishes of the company's management

I

indemnity, (1) an agreement that protects against damage or loss; (2) the compensation granted for the loss, up to the insurance policy's face value

indenture, (1) a written agreement that establishes the conditions of a bond issue and authorizes an independent trustee to act on behalf of the bondholders; (2) a deed including several parties; (3) a contract that binds the labor of a person to an employer for a stated period

individual retirement account (IRA), a plan whereby a person can put a percentage of income into a fund which is exempt from tax as income or earnings until the person's retirement

interface, (1) the connection or coordination between two or more systems; (2) the boundary between parts or systems

inventory, (1) a list of all items owned by a person or firm and their value; (2) raw material, products in process, and finished goods scheduled for use or for sale

J-K

job description, a listing of the qualifications and obligations for a specific position

job shop, a producer who makes custom orders rather than items for general inventory

junk bond, a high-risk, high-interest bearing bond issued by a company that is attempting to raise capital quickly

L

letter of credit, a letter from a bank that requests other institutions to extend credit or advance money to the holder and guarantees reimbursement

leverage, financial speculation using borrowed capital with the expectation that future profits will be greater than interest payments

liability, (1) debt owed; (2) an obligation by a person or company that is subject to a claim

license, a permit granted by a government, person, or institution to do certain acts or to conduct a specific business

lien, a legal right claimed by a creditor against the property of a debtor

limited, (1) a corporation where shareholders' liability is confined to the amount of their investment; (2) a corporation, chiefly in British usage

limited partnership, ownership in a business by investment only, with no role in management and with liability restricted to the size of investment

line of credit, the maximum amount that a lending institution will lend to a borrower

liquid assets, assets that are cash or that can be readily converted to cash

liquidation, (1) conversion of assets to cash either to take a profit or terminate a business; (2) fulfillment of an obligation, such as repaying a loan

loss leader, merchandise sold below cost to attract customers

M

margin, (1) the difference between the price paid and the price sold; (2) to buy a security with a loan from a broker as partial payment

market price, (1) the prevailing price of an item at the time; (2) the price established by supply and demand; (3) the last price quoted for a security when traded

merger, the uniting of two or more businesses under the ownership of the firm that acquires the stock of the other business(es)

money market, the system through which transactions are made in short-term funds such as loans, gold, securities, or foreign currencies

money market fund, a mutual fund that deals with short-term securities

moratorium, a period, granted legally, in which a debtor is permitted to delay payment of an obligation beyond the date due

mortgage, a legal arrangement that places title in real estate or property as security for payment of a loan

multinational company, a company that operates in a global market with management centers, production facilities, and assets in several countries

municipal bond, a bond issued by a local government

mutual company, a corporation without stock whose officers are elected and whose profits are shared by policy-holders or members according to their amount of business, as with mutual insurance companies or mutual savings banks

mutual fund, an open-end investment trust which issues shares by customer demand and gives management broad power to select investments

N

negotiable, documents that can be transferred from one person to another through endorsement or other legal strictures

net assets, working capital, the amount that remains after deductions for liabilities

O

odd lot, in commodity and security sales, an amount that differs from the customary trading unit, i.e., less than 100 shares of stock

offer, contract terms proposed by one party (offeror) to another party (offeree)

open shop, a business that employs union and nonunion workers on equal terms

opening price, the amount of the first sale of a security on a market day

option, (1) a legally binding promise to keep an offer open for a specific period; (2) a right to buy or sell a property within a specific period; (3) alternatives available after discontinuing payment of insurance premiums

overdraft, the amount that a demand for payment, such as a check, exceeds the balance of funds on deposit

over-the-counter, securities transactions that occur outside regular stock exchanges, whether or not the security is listed on an exchange

P

paper profit, a profit that would be obtained if a security or property were actually sold rather than retained

parity price, a sum paid to American farmers for their produce to protect their purchasing power

patent, an exclusive right granted by a government to the inventor to manufacture, use, or sell an invention for a specific period

payback period, the estimated time required to recover the cost of a capital investment

per capita, Latin for "by head," that is, for each person

petty cash, a limited cash fund used for minor expenses

posting, transferring entries from a journal to a ledger in accounting

power of attorney, a document that authorizes an agent to act on one's behalf

predating, affixing a date to a document earlier than it was signed

preferred stock, stock entitling the holder to receive dividends and assets upon liquidation before the holders of common stock

premium, (1) the sum a policyholder pays for an insurance policy; (2) a bonus or special payment in goods, services, or cash; (3) the difference between the price of a stock or bond and its face value

price fixing, the regulation of prices by agreement of private persons or firms, usually illegally, or legally by the government

price index, a table that indicates the relative change in the price of an item over time, expressed as a ratio

prime rate, the interest rate that a bank charges to its best customers for short-term loans

principal, (1) a person who is represented by an agent; (2) the sum of capital loaned or invested, distinguished from interest or profits

productivity, the quantity of output by one factor (e.g., a worker) over a unit of time

profit, (1) the amount that revenues exceed the costs of obtaining revenues; (2) the amount earned beyond capital investment when prices of goods sold exceed cost of production

profit margin, a ratio or percentage indicating the relation between gross profit and net sales

profit sharing, distribution of a share of a business' profits to its employees in addition to wages

progressive tax, a tax levied at increasingly higher rates as the income level or the tax base becomes higher

promissory note, a written promise to pay a specific sum to a particular person (often the bearer) on a certain date or on demand

property tax, a tax levied on personal articles owned or on land and buildings

probate, judicial process that verifies and registers the legitimacy of a last will and testament after death

prorate, (1) to apportion a cost over an account according to some system of distribution; (2) to distribute the total amount of insurance over several items in proportion to their value

prospectus, a statement from a corporation containing financial details and data about an offer of securities

proxy, a written statement from a shareholder authorizing another person to represent and vote on behalf of the shareholder

pump priming, large governmental expenditures to stimulate economic growth through increased purchase power and employment

purchasing power, the value of money according to its ability to buy goods

Q

quality control, the system necessary to insure that a company's goods or services meet minimum standards

R

rate of return, (1) the rate of earned profit compared to the amount of capital invested; (2) a rate permitted by a regulatory agency to a public utility to insure fair profit on capital investment and to protect consumers

real cost, (1) the cost after compensating for changes in purchasing power; (2) the cost when compared to other uses of the same money; (3) the cost in concrete terms of measurement such as tons, square feet, labor hours, etc.

real estate, land with buildings, fences, or other immovable improvements

real property, land, buildings, and improvements in contrast to personal property

receiver, a person appointed by a court to administer impartially disputed funds or property by reason of debt

receivership, a legal action entailing a court's appointment of an impartial manager to administer the funds and property of a person or firm unable to pay debts

redemption, (1) the repurchase of a note, stock, bond, or currency by the issuing agency, usually for cash; (2) after foreclosure, the freeing of the mortgage lien by payment of obligations past due

registrar, a person who signs stock certificates and ensures that the stock is authorized by the issuing company

repurchase agreement, the sale of securities on a temporary basis with the seller agreeing to buy them back after an agreed time

reserves, (1) the funds set aside from profits for the payment of debt or other need; (2) funds an insurer uses to meet claims and other liabilities

resources, assets

retail, the sale of goods directly to consumers for final consumption

return, profit rate relative to the value of capital invested

risk, the probability of loss or profit of an investment

round lot, a conventional trading unit, such as 100 shares of stock or $1000 par value for bonds

royalty, a price paid in return for a right—to an author for a book, to a landowner to mine, to a patent holder to manufacture, and so on

S

sale, (1) the transfer of title of ownership of property for a price; (2) the chance to buy goods at a reduced price

salvage, (1) the value of an item for other than original use or for resale; (2) in insurance, the value of property after it has sustained damage

saturation point, a market whose potential has been fully exploited

security, (1) a written instrument that indicates indebtedness or ownership, such as a bond, stock, bill, mortgage, receipt, and so on; (2) a pledge made to a lender that assures repayment of a loan

self-liquidating, a loan or investment that yields a return sufficient to pay for itself

sell short, to sell a security or commodity not actually owned in anticipation of a decline in price

seller's market, a market where demand exceeds supply, hence sellers can control prices or terms of sale

settlement, (1) resolution of a dispute outside of court; (2) completion of a financial obligation

share, a unit or portion of ownership in a business

silent partner, a person who invests in a partnership but does not actively participate in management

simple interest, interest paid on the principal only, not on accumulated interest

sinking fund, a sum consisting of moneys set aside regularly and usually invested at interest to pay debts, redeem bonds, meet expenses, and so on

slowdown, a deliberate reduction in the rate of production by management or (more often) by labor

solvency, (1) the ability of a business to meet its obligations when due; (2) the condition wherein a business' total assets exceed its total liabilities

speculation, sales or purchases of goods or securities with the intent of quick profit rather than long-term investment

stock, (1) a share of ownership in a corporation; (2) the certificate itself representing the share; (3) the total sum of capital invested in the business; (4) merchandise a company holds for sale and the materials necessary for a business to finish that merchandise

stock exchange, a market where brokers buy and sell stocks and bonds during certain hours and under proscribed rules

stop order, an order to buy or sell a specified number of shares of a security when the market price reaches a certain level

stop payment, a depositor's order to a bank not to make payment on a certain stock

subsidy, a governmental grant to a person, firm, or industry to encourage productivity or to support an effort beneficial to the public

supply, the producer's readiness to sell a certain quantity of goods or services at a specified price, time, and market

surety bond, a form of insurance wherein a third party (the surety) promises to reimburse the insured party named in the bond against the default of another party (the principal)

surplus, (1) the excess of revenue over expenditure; (2) earnings from production beyond the cost of production; (3) an excess of products over market demand

surtax, an extra tax beyond the normal rate

T

tangible assets, (1) resources that are substantial, such as real estate; (2) resources including stock, property, or cash as opposed to such intangible assets as goodwill, rights, or patents

tariff, (1) a customs tax on goods as they enter or (less often) leave a country; (2) a schedule of rates, changes or rules, usually of transportation

tender, (1) an offer to pay money, perform a service, or deliver goods; (2) a means to acquire control of a corporation by asking shareholders to sell their stock at a fixed price by a certain date

time deposit, a bank deposit that cannot be withdrawn before a specified time or without advanced notice

title, a document that gives evidence of ownership

trading down, buying and selling lower-priced merchandise to increase profits through higher sales volume

trading up, buying and selling higher-priced merchandise to increase the profit margin

transfer agent, a person who records transactions of a company's stock and is responsible for issuing shares and keeping records of shareholders

trust, (1) a legal procedure in which one party (the trustee) holds title to a property for the benefit of another party (the beneficiary); (2) an association or corporation with a single board of trustees that exercises a monopoly on the production and distribution of a good or service

turnover, (1) the number of times a cycle repeats itself in a given period; (2) the number of workers hired to replace those who leave relative to the total number of workers; (3) sale of goods

U-Z

underwriter, a person or organization that guarantees a risk against losses, especially in insurance and investment of stocks

unlisted security, a security traded over the counter and not negotiated on a recognized stock exchange

venture capital, a risky or speculative investment for the forming of new businesses, particularly small ones

warrant, (1) a legal document authorizing arrest; (2) a certificate granting an option to purchase stock at a specified price within a stated period

warranty, a guarantee that certain facts are true as represented

wholesale, buying and selling by a middleman to retailers or to major commercial users, but rarely to the ultimate consumers

write-off, an accounting procedure to compensate for bad debts or losses by balancing them against earnings or other funds

yield, (1) rate of return as a percentage; (2) the ratio between the dividend of a stock and its purchase price